A Book in Hand Is Worth
Two in the Library

A Book in Hand Is Worth Two in the Library

Quotations on Books and Librarianship

by LES HARDING

McFarland & Company, Inc., Publishers
Jefferson, North Carolina, and London

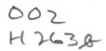

British Library Cataloguing-in-Publication data are available

Library of Congress Cataloguing-in-Publication Data

Harding, Les, 1950–
    A book in hand is worth two in the library : quotations on books
and librarianship / by Les Harding.
        p.   cm.
    Includes index.
    ISBN 0-89950-933-9 (sewn softcover : 55# alk. paper) ∞
    1. Books and reading – Quotations, maxims, etc.   2. Library
science – Quotations, maxims, etc.   I. Title.
PN6084.B65H37   1994
002 – dc20   93-42599
                                                                         CIP

Manufactured in the United States of America

McFarland & Company, Inc., Publishers
  Box 611, Jefferson, North Carolina 28640

Acknowledgments

Acknowledgment is hereby gratefully made to the following authors, their representatives, and publishing houses who permitted the use of copyrighted material.

A. P. Watt Ltd., on behalf of The Royal Literary Fund, for a quote from **The Summing Up,** by W. Somerset Maugham.

Peters Fraser & Dunlop Group Ltd. for quotes from Hilaire Belloc's **On the Gift of a Book to a Child.**

Quotes from **Crisis at the Victory Burlesk,** by Robert Fulford. Copyright Oxford University Press Canada 1968. Reprinted by permission of the publisher.

Random House Inc. for a quote from H. L. Mencken's **Minority Report: H. L. Mencken's Notebooks.**

Blackwell Publishers for a quote from George Leslie Brook's **Books and Book Collecting.**

Peters Fraser & Dunlop Group Ltd., on behalf of the estate of Evelyn Waugh, for a quote from Evelyn Waugh's **Vile Bodies.**

Macmillan Publishing Company for a quote from Josephine Tey's **The Singing Sands,** 1952.

Reed International Books and William Heinemann Ltd. for a quote from Max Beerbohm's **Zuleika Dobson.**

Longman Group UK Ltd. for a quote from G. M. Trevelyan's **English Social History.**

For a quote from Walter Hart Blumenthal's **Bookmen's Bedlam.** From "The Folklore and Folklife of New Jersey" by David S. Cohen, Copyright by Rutgers, The State University.

Books for Libraries Press, Ayer Co. Publishers, Inc., for a quote from Abraham Simon Wolf Rosenbach's **A Book Hunter's Holiday.**

Farley Mowat Ltd. for a quote from Farley Mowat's **The Dog Who Wouldn't Be.**

Robertson Davies for quotes from his **Fifth Business,** and **A Voice from the Attic.**

Quote from **Tempest Tost** by Robertson Davies. Copyright Clarke, Irwin & Co. Ltd. 1951. Reprinted by permission of Penguin Books Canada Ltd.

Excerpt from "England Your England" in **Such, Such Were the Joys,** by George Orwell, copyright 1953 by Sonia Brownell Orwell and renewed 1981 by Mrs. George K. Perutz, Mrs. Miriam Goss and Dr. Michael Dickson, Executors of the Estate of Sonia Brownell Orwell, reprinted by permission of Harcourt Brace & Company.

Quote from **Freedom at Midnight,** Copyright 1975 by Larry Collins and Dominique Lapierre. Reprinted by permission of Simon & Schuster, Inc.

For a quote from **Cultural Comparisons of England with America,** Copyright 1977 by Martin Green, Harper Collins Publishers.

With the permission of Taiyi Lin Lai and Hsiang Ju Lin for quotes by Lin Yutang.

Quotes by Georgie Starbuck and P. Nicholson reprinted from **Bartlett's Unfamiliar Quotations,** by Leonard E. Levinson, 1971. Used with permission of Contemporary Books, Inc., Chicago.

Contents

Acknowledgments   *v*

Preface   *1*

1 Libraries   7

2 Librarians   *23*

3 Books   *31*

4 Bookworms   *47*

5 Borrowing and Lending   *57*

6 Censorship   *69*

7 Classics   *77*

8 Reading   *83*

9 Writing   *93*

10 Education   *101*

Conclusion   *109*

Indices   *111*

    Speaker/Writer Index   *113*

    Key Word & Subject Index   *117*

Preface

"I like prefaces. I read them. Sometimes I do not read any further."
— Malcolm Lowry (1909–1957)

Recently, upon browsing through some thick and dusty tomes — dictionaries of quotations, collections of proverbs, after-dinner stories, advice for the toastmaster, wise and witty sayings, humorous headstones, facetiae, maxims, anecdotes, and the like — I chanced upon a page bearing the curious heading *Libraries and Librarians*. Eager to see what the great minds of the past and present have had to say about the profession with which I have had some tenuous connection, I polished my glasses with the end of my shirt, and peered closer. The first quotation was . . . interesting.

"A circulating library is an evergreen tree of
diabolical knowledge."
— RICHARD BRINSLEY SHERIDAN (1751–1816)

Perplexed, and somewhat startled by the severity of that comment, I continued foraging. The next three quotations were even more . . . interesting.

"Burn the libraries!"
— THE CALIPH OMAR (c. 581–644)

"A library makes me sick."
— FRIEDRICH NIETZSCHE (1844–1900)
(Nietzsche makes *me* sick! So there.)

"My son the librarian!"
— ANON.

At the end of the *Libraries and Librarians* section was a further reference, *See: Books, Bookworms, Borrowing and Lending, Censorship, Classics, Reading, Writing, and Education.* With this I started off on a minor odyssey of sorts. The library/librarian remarks set the tone for what was to follow.

Books

"'Tis pleasant, sure, to see one's name in print;
A book's a book, although there's nothing in't."
— LORD BYRON (1788–1824)

Bookworms

"A bookworm is a person who would rather read than eat, or it is a worm that would rather eat than read."
— ANON.

Borrowing and Lending

"Borrowers of books — those mutilators of collections, spoilers of the symmetry of shelves, and creators of odd volumes."
— CHARLES LAMB (1775–1834)

Censorship

"Particularly against books the Home Secretary is. If we can't stamp out literature in the country we can at least stop it from being brought in from outside."
— EVELYN WAUGH (1903–1966)

Classics

"A classic is something that everybody wants to *have* read and nobody wants to *read*."
— MARK TWAIN (1835–1910)

Reading

"Reading rots the brain."
— NEW ENGLAND PROVERB

Writing

"Don't be afraid! We won't make an author of you; while there's an honest trade to be learnt, or brickmaking to turn to."
— CHARLES DICKENS (1812–1870)

Education

"Soap and education are not as sudden as a massacre, but they are more deadly in the long run."
— MARK TWAIN (1835–1910)

The results of my gleanings, supplemented by a considerable amount of literary detective work and serendipitous reading, are in your hands. I urge you, gentle readers, to treat this work with the respect it deserves.

"Child! Do not throw this book about;
Refrain from the unholy pleasure
Of cutting all the pictures out!
Preserve it as your chiefest treasure.
Child, have you never heard it said
That you are heir to all the ages?
Why, then, your hands were never made
To tear these beautiful thick pages!"
— HILAIRE BELLOC (1870–1953)

There was one additional heading I could not help but look under — *Quotations.* Here I discovered what may be the most germane quotations of all for setting this book in its proper light.

"I hate quotations."
— RALPH WALDO EMERSON (1803–1882)

"A book that furnishes me with no quotation is
. . . no book — it is a plaything."
— THOMAS LOVE PEACOCK (1785–1866)

"Let it not be said that I have said
nothing new. The arrangement of the
material is new."
— BLAISE PASCAL (1623–1662)

1

Libraries

"Th' first thing to have in a library is a
shelf. Fr'm time to time this can be decorated with lithrachure. But th' shelf is the
main thing."
    —Finley Peter Dunne (1867–1936)

People who are in love with books (almost never librarians) can be brought to the heights of ecstasy by the thought of an entire library just waiting to be browsed. The enthusiasm such persons feel for libraries tends to run away with them. Their praise becomes a little too verbose for my taste.

> "I go into my library and all history rolls
> before me. I breathe the morning air of the
> world while the scent of Eden's roses yet
> lingered in it . . . I see the pyramids building; I
> hear the shoutings of the armies of Alexander
> . . . I sit as in a theatre — the stage is time, the
> play is the play of the world."
> — ALEXANDER SMITH (1830–1867)

In my time I have plunged my flaring nostrils into more than one shelf list but I have yet to be rewarded with so much as a wisp of Eden's roses — just sneezes.

> "What a place to be is an old library! It seems
> as though all the souls of all the writers, that
> have bequeathed their labours to these Bodle-
> ians, were reposing here, as in some dormitory,
> or middle state. I do not want to handle, to
> profane their leaves, their winding sheets. I
> could as soon dislodge a shade. I seem to in-
> hale learning, walking amid their foliage; and
> the odour of their old moth-scented coverings
> is fragrant as the first bloom of those sciential
> apples which grew amid the happy orchard."
> — CHARLES LAMB (1775–1834)

Again with the fragrances! I would not advise any library user of today to go around sniffing blooming sciential apples, unless first checking that library security is not in view. The pleasure library lovers obtain as they crack a good binding, tease a treatise, cuddle a codex, or fondle a fly-leaf can approach the erotic.

"A man's library is a sort of harem."
— RALPH WALDO EMERSON (1803–1882)

Decorum, of course, should always be upheld.

"Lady Gough, assured herself a measure
of immortality by forbidding the placing
of books by male authors in her library
alongside books by female authors —
unless, of course, they were married."
— W. HART BLUMENTHAL (1883–1969)

"There is something very undignified about
being caught making out in a library."
— ELIZABETH PETERS (1927–   )

Most people, including those who respect and cherish books
(almost no one respects and cherishes microforms), see a library
in a much more somber light. A library can be a place tinged with
sadness and failed dreams.

"A library is but the soul's burial-ground."
— HENRY WARD BEECHER (1813–1887)

"Shelved around us lie the mummified
authors."
— BAYARD TAYLOR (1825–1878)

"Look at the back stacks of any great
library, what a necropolis of immortals in
there."
— GOLDWIN SMITH (1823–1910)

"What laborious days, what watchings by
the midnight lamp, what racking of the
brain, what hopes and fears, what long
lives of laborious study are here subli-
mized into print, and condensed into the
narrow compass of these surrounding
shelves."
— HORACE SMITH (1779–1849)

"The dust and silence of the upper shelf."
— THOMAS BABINGTON MACAULAY
(1800–1859)

"For myself, public libraries possess a
special horror, as of lonely wastes and
dragon-haunted fens. The stillness and the
heavy air, the feeling of restriction and
surveillance, the mute presence of these
other readers, 'all silent and damned,'
combine to set up a nervous irritation
fatal to quiet study."
— KENNETH GRAHAME (1859–1932)

It is only recently that the right to use a library has been just
that — a right. Throughout most of history, library use was a
rarely granted privilege.

"Let no profane person enter!"
— ANON. (Inscription on an old
Swiss library.)

"A reader and a talker cannot agree;
hence, idle chatterer: 'tis no place for
thee."
— ISIDORE, BISHOP OF SEVILLE
(c. 560–636)

The earliest libraries were accumulations of baked clay
tablets and rolls of papyrus housed in the temple archives of
Mesopotamia and Egypt. Collections primarily comprised religious texts, which recounted the doings of the gods, while not
forgetting the glories of the reigning monarch. Also included were
records of commercial transactions, deeds of ownership, genealo-
gies, poetry, administrative documents, treatises on astrology,
medicine or agriculture, as well as catalogues of strange plants,
stranger people, marvelous animals, and wonders.

The library at Ninevah, in Assyria, was the first great library
in ancient times. It was established by Assurbanipal sometime in

the seventh century B.C. After having his priests suitably bless, cleanse and purify the premises, under the demanding eye (or eyes?) of Great Nabu, god of writing and things literary, Assurbanipal ordered the royal minions, who exhibited the tenacity of modern students queuing before a library's photocopier, to mount their asses and travel the length of the country copying, translating and — if required — thieving any writings they discovered. In no time, the holdings of the Ninevah Public Library were built up to a respectable 25,000 tablets. Such was the state of copyright at the time that the king affixed the royal signature to each and every one.

Each room in Assurbanipal's library contained works on a different subject. Tablets were kept in jars, and the jars on shelves. Each tablet was identified as to jar, shelf and room. The catalog was a simple list of each room's contents. It was painted or carved beside the entrance. Assyrian libraries practiced the closed jar system. If a user, usually a priest or minion, needed some information on, say, wonders, he would go to the wonders room, consult the catalog ("Hmmm, let me see, *Wonders of the West* by Assurbanipal, *Wonders of the South* principally edited by Assurbanipal, *Wonders of the North* inspired by ..." etc.) until he found the tablet he was interested in. The user was encouraged to write down the tablet number and present this information to the librarian, another priest/minion, who, if threatened in a nice way, would fetch the item.

As mentioned by that well-known first century Roman historian (and father of the air freshener!) Diodorous Siculus, the oldest library of consequence in Egypt was the one constructed at Thebes by Ramses II. This king is known to us as Ozymandius, thanks to Shelley's famous poem.* The library, again mostly religious and philosophical in nature, was called, somewhat grandly, "A Sanatorium for the Mind." It was adorned with a massive statue of its benefactor, inscribed, "I am Ozymandius, King of Kings."

Meanwhile, in Greece, Athens may have had a reading

---

*Recent archaeological excavations have suggested that Ozymandius may have sired a hermaphrodite offspring, Ozzyanharrietus.

public, and a library to serve it, as early as 560 B.C. The tyrant Pisistratus was a dedicated collector (read: thief) of manuscripts and soon needed a place to store his loot. It was in Greece that the idea of a library as a collection of books for reading and study really originated. During the lifetime of Aristotle (c. 384–322 B.C.), the Greek world passed from an oral, briefly to an anal, and finally to a written culture. Academies were founded and funding drives were started to provide their libraries with books. The drives were not quite the same as the library fund raisers of today. "A hundred drachma and we do not break your legs," was a typical request for funds, as was "50 drachma in a brown parchment bag, or your little friend the sheep returns to the hillside." It was in this manner, historians believe, that Aristotle amassed one of the largest private libraries in antiquity. That sly old Stagirite had several hundred volumes in his possession, curiously including not a few once owned by his teacher, Plato.

The greatest library in the classical world was the famous Greek library at Alexandria. Founded by Ptolemy II in 300 B.C., it established itself as the foremost center for scholarship. The Alexandria library set out to collect the finest copies of every known book. To this end, scribes were dispatched to every country to seek out manuscripts. Deposits were left for borrowed books. Sometimes "deposits" were left *on* borrowed books. If the book was deemed to be of sufficient importance, the deposit was conveniently forgotten and the book kept. So intense was the drive to have every book ever written, that ships docking at the port of Alexandria were forbidden to sail until they were searched for books. Any books they contained would then be copied or seized. Matters got out of hand when papyrus supplies to rival libraries were cut off. The librarians at Alexandria wanted to ensure that their library would have not just every book that had been written, but every book that ever *would* be written. Eventually, the library obtained from Athens the official stage copies of the works of the great tragedians.

In the days of Sophocles and Euripides, sanctioned copies of plays had been placed in a public collection. A copyright collection of manuscripts, which became a sort of public library, was needed to verify the accuracy of the texts. By the end of the third century B.C. libraries were common throughout Greece. Athenian libraries were kept clean and inviting — so much so that one scholar spent fifty years of his life reading through them.

With the rise of Rome, entire Greek libraries, and many unfortunate Greek librarians, were strapped to mules and carted off to Italy as war booty. Books, as well as librarians, often ended up as part of huge private collections. Aristotle's library is said to have met this fate. Book collecting became something of a craze among the Roman upper crust, even among those who could not read. Such persons were referred to as "book clowns."

> "Nowadays a library takes rank with a bathroom as a necessary ornament of a house."
> — SENECA (c. 4 B.C.–A.D. 65)

No villa was considered complete without its fine library of bookcases. There were private collections of twenty, forty, and even sixty thousand rolls! Cicero, to whom a library was "the soul of his house," was only one of many who felt contempt for him who stuffs his house with literature yet "hardly reads the titles." The Stoics, who frowned upon the owning of property of any kind, were quick to denounce the extravagances they saw in others.

> "Since you cannot read all the books which you may possess, it is enough to possess only as many as you can read."
> — SENECA (c. 4 B.C.–A.D. 65)

Private libraries varied in splendor according to the means of the owner. The important thing was that the collection, no matter how small, be displayed to advantage.

> "O library of a dainty country house ... thou mayest put in a niche, though it be the lowest one, these seven little books which I have sent thee."
> — MARTIAL (c. 40–c. A.D. 104)

Julius Caesar was the first to plan a public library. Naturally, as befitting the dignity and grandeur of Rome, it would have to be much more splendid than the library of Alexandria. Unfortunately, events of the Ides of March interfered with Caesar's plans. To Asinius Pollio (whose name, if read quickly, resembles an asinine disease) was left the honor of being the first person of whom it could be said, "He made men's tablets public property." No matter that most writing was in the form of scrolls; we are speaking metaphorically.

Not to be outdone by such a one as Asinius, the emperor Augustus established *two* libraries. As with book collecting, so with public libraries. They became the rage. After Augustus, most emperors and many wealthy citizens founded public libraries. Pliny the Younger started his library in the hope that it would keep the young men from gambling, drinking, and the curse of sport. It is not likely that he was successful in his aim.

> "Libries niver encouraged lithrachoor, any
> more than tombstones encourage livin'."
> — FINLEY PETER DUNNE (1867–1936)

The Roman public libraries, though open to anyone, freeman or slave, who could read, remained under private control. That the public was permitted access was a positive reflection of the owner's greatness and magnanimity. Libraries were often associated with temples and patrons lavishly decorated them with statuary and art. By the fourth century there were twenty-eight libraries in the city of Rome and others in the provinces.

The typical Roman library was split into two sections — Greek and Latin. Books, still mostly rolls, were arranged according to subject, on shelves or in bins. The library building usually faced west to take full advantage of the morning light and help preserve the papyrus from dampness. This was a constant battle. Few things in life could have been more unpleasant than to be exposed to a library full of damp moldy papyrus rolls. An attempt was made to control the amount of moisture by encasing book compartments between double walls.

Beginning in the fifth century, the civilization of Rome was swept away by barbarian hordes. Manuscripts, so carefully preserved for centuries, were used to clean boots and start campfires. For one thousand years, from Greece to Iceland, the typical library was reduced to a chest of books in a monastery. Five hundred volumes was an unusually large collection.

At the same time, the Moslem world was experiencing a flowering of culture and learning. A library in Moslem Spain contained 400,000 volumes and employed five hundred scribes! Cairo, in the eleventh century, was said to have 1,200,000 books in its libraries. A tenth century Baghdad scholar, Abdul Kessem Ismael, would never travel anywhere without his 117,000 books. In order to be able to find anything he wanted, he had four hundred camels trained to walk in alphabetical order.

In Christian Europe manuscripts were very expensive and difficult to reproduce. Only a very rich man could afford to buy a Bible. Books were as prized as they were rare.

"A monastery without a book-chest is like a castle without an armory."
— Twelfth century aphorism

In the sixth century, the first scriptorium for the copying of books was established in a monastery. The copying of books, by hand, was a tedious operation. The copiers stood — or, if they were lucky, sat — in front of sloping desks and scribed away for months and years on end. Plain parchment was used, sometimes dyed, with many varieties of colored inks. A good scribe could complete five book-sized pages in a day. Working at that pace it took approximately one year to copy out the Bible. The work was not over then. A completed manuscript had to be checked by a second monk for accuracy, and the inevitable corrections made. Finally, the book would be given to a third monk for illumination — decorative lettering and ornamentation.

Monastery books started out plain but became more elaborate with the passage of time. Margins were decorated and title pages added with ornamental borders and miniature paintings. The parchment might be dyed purple or green and the entire work lettered in gold and silver. The best efforts of the monks often fell on blind eyes.

> "There is a class of thieves shamefully mutilat-
> ing books, who cut away the margins from the
> sides to use as material for letters, leaving only
> the text, or employ the leaves from the ends,
> inserted for the protection of the book, for
> various uses and abuses — a kind of sacrilege
> which should be prohibited by the threat of
> anathema."
> — RICHARD DE BURY (1287–1345)

In the later Middle Ages, monastic libraries diminished in importance. The nobility and the bourgeoisie in the towns began collecting books for their own amusement and instruction. Queen Isabel of France (1370–1435) was so burdened with books that one of her ladies-in-waiting was pressed into service as her personal librarian. The third duke of Burgundy (1396–1467) was a bookman of such magnitude that he employed his own copyists, translators and illuminators. It was his ambition to have the grandest library in the world.

The Medici family were the first great patrons of libraries in the Renaissance. Cosimo de Medici started the first public library in Europe since the days of the Roman Empire. The Medici bank provided a fanatic book collector, Niccolò de Niccoli, with an unlimited overdraft to indulge his passion. Upon his death, all outstanding debts were canceled in exchange for Niccoli's eight hundred book library. This collection was then donated to the city of Florence. Tomasso Parentucelli, the man hired to catalog the library, was later to shape the Vatican Library as Pope Nicolas V. Cosimo's grandson, Lorenzo de Medici, continued the family's interest in libraries. He was also one of the first book collectors in Europe to accept printed books in his library.

In England the monastic communities were decimated by Henry VIII. A similar fate befell many monasteries in Europe during the religious wars of the sixteenth century. Little attempt was made to protect the libraries of those monasteries. A feature of the seventeenth century was a revival of the great private book collector. As a result, much of what was scattered in the turmoil of the previous century was preserved. From their labors came the core from which the great university and national libraries arose.

"Did you read this in the paper this morning?
There are 800 people (get that, eight hundred)
at work in the Library of Congress.... Why
that's a librarian to each book."
— WILL ROGERS (1879–1935)

Early in the eighteenth century, booksellers hit upon a brilliant idea. Sick and tired of people who browsed but did not buy, they decided to start their own libraries and charge people to use them. The idea was an instant hit. The first circulating library was started in Edinburgh in 1740. Soon others sprouted up. They were particularly popular in health resorts and sanatoriums. By 1850 there were four hundred circulating libraries. Essentially they were rental collections, providing popular reading for a small fee. A bookseller who started such a library could then, conveniently, publish the popular fiction to fill it. Circulating libraries grew to have an enormous influence over the taste of popular reading. As much as three quarters of the sales of a popular novel would be taken up by the circulating libraries.

Because they appealed strictly to the popular taste, circulating libraries were not without their detractors. The literary set were appalled.

"Slop Shops in Literature."
— ELIZABETH GRIFFITH (c. 1720–1793)

"For as to the devotees of the circulating
libraries I dare not compliment their pass-
time, or rather kill-time, with the name of
reading."
— SAMUEL TAYLOR COLERIDGE
(1772–1834)

Part of the problem, a problem which writers still face, was that every time a book circulated in the libraries the author was losing a sale.

> "We call ourselves a rich nation, and we are
> filthy enough and foolish enough to thumb
> each other's books out of circulating libraries."
> —JOHN RUSKIN (1819–1900)

Circulating libraries endured and paved the way for the modern public library, the first of which was the Manchester Free Library, opened in 1852.

> "What a sad want of libraries, of books to
> gather facts from! Why is there not a Majesty's
> library in every county town? There is a Maj-
> esty's gaol in every one."
> —THOMAS CARLYLE (1795–1881)

Since that time, most municipalities have felt obliged to provide their citizens with a library of some sort.

> "It was not much of a collection—perhaps
> fifteen hundred books in all, of which
> roughly a tenth part were for children.
> The annual budget was twenty-five dol-
> lars, and much of that went on subscrip-
> tions to magazines that the magistrate,
> who was chairman of the board, wanted
> to read."
> —ROBERTSON DAVIES (1913–)

> "This is a quite dowdy institution, con-
> taining many symbols of the Victorian
> past and many symbols of continuance in
> service, like a photograph of an assistant
> librarian who spent seventy years there
> from 1882 to 1952."
> —MARTIN GREEN (1927–)

"Acquisitions, therefore, were usually gifts
from the estates of people who had died, and
our local auctioneer gave us any books that he
could not sell; we kept what we wanted and
sent the rest to the Grenfell Mission, on the
principle that savages would read anything."
— ROBERTSON DAVIES (1913–)

But do you think those citizens are grateful for their library
service?

"There are 70,000,000 books in American
libraries but the one you want to read is
always out."
— TOM MASSON (1866–1934)

"My experience with public libraries is
that the first volume of the book I inquire for is out, unless I happen to
want the second, when *that* is out."
— OLIVER WENDELL HOLMES
(1809–1894)

"There are too many books in every
public library and not enough people to
dust them."
— ANON.

Sometimes the citizenry dare to provide advice to the librarians!

"Every library should try to be complete
on something, if it were only the history
of pinheads."
— OLIVER WENDELL HOLMES
(1809–1894)

"Just the omission of Jane Austen's books
alone would make a fairly good library
out of a library that hadn't a book in it."
— MARK TWAIN (1835–1910)

Finally, some concluding statements on libraries.

"What do we as a nation care about
books? How much do you think we
spend altogether on our libraries, public
or private, as compared with what we
spend on our horses?"
— JOHN RUSKIN (1819–1900)

"I love libraries, but I will be damned if I
will ever walk into a 'Resource Centre.'"
— RICHARD NEEDHAM (1912–   )

2

Librarians

"The librarian who looks upon the ever
moving throng of book users only as an
unending influx of unreasonable or stupid
consumers of the trivial and commonplace
should find another vocation."
— HELEN HAINES (1872–1961)

As early as 3,000 B.C. there were men entitled "Keepers of the Scrolls," "Scribes of the Double House of Life," "Learned of the Magic Library." There were women as well: "Lady of Letters," "Mistress of the House of Books." The first librarian known by name is a Mr. Amit Anu, of the Royal Library at Ur, in 2000 B.C. He was followed by Amen-em-hant, chief librarian at Thebes for Pharaoh Ramses II. Since those times, such disparate individuals as August Strindberg, Mao Tse-Tung, Leibniz, Immanuel Kant, Henry Wadsworth Longfellow, the brothers Grimm, Goethe, Benjamin Franklin, Casanova, Arthur Evans, David Hume, Hector Berlioz, Freidrich Engels, Jorge Luis Borges, John Braine, J. Edgar Hoover, and at least five popes have been librarians.

Despite their often high sounding titles, the earliest librarians (and here we mean to cast no aspersions on the memory of Amit Anu and Amen-em-hant) were usually the younger half-wit sons or unmarriageable daughters of the lesser nobility. The Roman librarian was often an educated slave or a prisoner of war from Greece. In the Middle Ages, librarians tended to be monks, charitably described as elderly, crippled and infirm, and sometimes nearly blind as well. Librarians at the universities were minor, overworked faculty members or (shudder) students.

> "Librarie-Keepers, in most Universities . . . are but mercenaire and their employment of little or no use further, than to look to the Books committed to their custodie that they may not bee lost; or embezzled by those that use them: and that is all."
> —JOHN DURY (1596–1680)

With librarians of that stature, it should come as no surprise that the stock of books was often pawned or sold to pay personal debts.

By contrast the librarian of today is most often a disgruntled arts graduate who can find no honest employment anywhere else.

The library user, or patron . . .

"Patron: One who countenances, supports or
protects. Commonly a wretch who supports
with insolence, and is paid with flattery."
—SAMUEL JOHNSON (1709–1784)

...has seldom had a high opinion of librarians. To paraphrase
George Bernard Shaw's famous maxim:

"He who can, does.
He who cannot, shelves books."

Many library patrons have no idea just what it is that librarians do all day.

"Be you a library missionary, Miss?"
—JESSIE BEAUMONT MIFFLEN
(1906–   ) (Asked of a librarian
visiting a remote Newfoundland
community.)

"Miss Wallace just loved to sit there [The
Library of Congress] and read. It was so
quiet and so cool and so restful. But
wasn't it rather carrying coals to Newcastle to take a book along? They have, you
see, quite a few volumes already accumu-
lated at the Congressional. The librarians
there would let her have any one she
wanted. The mere suggestion agitated
Miss Wallace.
'I think,' she said with a subsiding flut-
ter, 'I'd rather take one along. I don't like
to bother them.'"
—ALEXANDER WOOLLCOTT (1887–1943)

Librarians get a bad press. Such has been the case throughout
history. They are seldom given the honor of being hated; librarians are not important enough for that distinction. The librarian
gets pitied more often than reviled.

"It is not observed that . . . librarians are wiser men than others."
RALPH WALDO EMERSON (1803–1882)

"Meek young men grow up in libraries."
— RALPH WALDO EMERSON (1803–1882)

"A great many readers are wholly insensitive to literary quality; to them, subject interest and moral acceptability are the only things that count. Comparatively few relate a book to its author, with any recognition of his style, his characteristics, his preceding work, and his status as a writer. Not all of these tendencies are confined to the public; some of them may be frequently observed in librarians."
— HELEN HAINES (1872–1961)

"Unlearned men of books assume the care,
As eunuchs are the guardians of the fair."
— EDWARD YOUNG (1683–1765)

By the eighteenth century, the librarian/eunuch connection had become something of a standard joke.

"A nobleman having chosen a very illiterate person for his library keeper said it was like a seraglio kept by an eunuch."
— JOHN MOTTLEY (1692–1750) (This questionable joke was taken from the first joke book in the English language, the basis of all modern humor — *Joe Miller's Jests or, the Wit's Vade-Mecum, being a collection of the most brilliant jests, the most polite repartees, the most elegant bon mots, the most pleasant short stories in the English language. First carefully collected in the company, and many of them transcribed from the mouth of the facetious gentleman whose name they bear.*

Despite their proximity to great quantities of learned books, librarians have been considered so stupid that every little thing has to be spelled out for them.

"Arrange them all in good order, so that
thou weary not in looking for a book
when thou needest it. . . . Write down the
titles of the books in each row of the
cases in a separate notebook and place
each in its row, in order that thou mayest
be able to see exactly in which row any
particular book is without mixing up the
others. Do the same with the cases. Look
continually into the catalog in order to
remember what books thou hast. When
thou lendest a book, record its title before
it leaves the house; and when it is
brought back draw thy pen through the
memorandum."
        — JUDA IBN TIBBON (1120–1170)

"Thou must have full knowledge of what
is given to thy charge. The first duty of a
librarian is to strive, in his time, as far as
possible, to increase the library com-
mitted to him. Let him beware that the
library does not diminish, that the books
in his charge do not in any way get lost
or perish. Let him repair by binding
books that are damaged by age. Let him
know the names of the authors."
        — RULES FOR AN ENGLISH MONASTIC
        LIBRARY.

The poor image of the librarian has survived to our own
time.

"Some of the bitterest arguments came over the
books in India's libraries. Sets of the Encyclopedia Britannica were religiously divided up,
alternate volumes to each dominion. Dictionaries
were ripped in half with A to K going to India,
the rest to Pakistan. Where only one copy of a
book was available, the librarians were supposed to decide which dominion would have

the greater natural interest in it. Some of those supposedly intelligent men actually came to blows arguing over which dominion had a greater natural interest in *Alice in Wonderland* and in *Wuthering Heights*."
   —LARRY COLLINS (1930–) and DOMINIQUE LAPIERRE (1932–) (A comment on the professionalism of India's librarians during the partition of the subcontinent in 1947.)

> "The proud mother was introducing her family to a visitor.
>   'Nine children,' exclaimed the visitor, 'and each one a librarian!'
>   'Not quite,' replied the mother. 'They're all librarians except Tommy, the little devil. He got to reading.'"
>   ANON. (Paraphrase of an old joke.)

Consider this description of the typical librarian.

> "The librarian was a thin little piece of faded elegance with a tie no broader than the black silk ribbon of his eyeglasses."
>   —JOSEPHINE TEY (1897–1952)

The only positive thing I could find about a librarian was by a man whose father was one.

> "Aaron looked at his mate with growing affection, and passed the bottle. 'By God, Angus,' he said, 'for a librarian you've got quite a brain.'"
>   —FARLEY MOWAT (1921–)

3

Books

"Something they make TV movies out of."
— Anon.

"A non-periodical printed publication of at least forty-nine pages excluding covers."
— UNESCO

Cadmus was a legendary Greek hero. He was ordered by his half-witted father to follow about after an exhausted cow until she dropped, at which point he was to found the city of Thebes with some handy dragon's teeth. Later, in one of his few lucid moments, Cadmus introduced the Phoenician alphabet to Greece. Cadmus spent his declining years in the Balkans as a highly respected serpent.

> "Blessings upon Cadmus, the Phoenicians, or whoever it was that invented books."
> —THOMAS CARLYLE (1795–1881)

Could such an eccentric person be the father of so noble a creation as the book? I think not. I hope not!

No one knows who invented the book, but it was probably some nameless Sumerian priest-librarian around 4000 B.C. Clay tablets were covered with wedge-shaped symbols called cuneiform and baked like bread. "Books" consisted of a series of numbered tablets stored in a labeled jar. The earliest best-seller that we know of was *The Gilgamesh,* an epic poem of the Flood which introduces such happy-go-lucky characters as Enkidu the Brute and Utnapishtim.

The use of papyrus as a writing material dates from 3500 B.C. in Egypt and later spread to Greece and Rome. The book was a papyrus roll. Papyrus was manufactured from strips torn not from the hide of a librarian, but from the pithy stems of the papyrus plant. In what sounds like some kind of weird college initiation rite, the strips were dyed, placed transversely atop one another, impregnated with glue, pressed tightly together and polished to a smooth writing surface with a block of ivory or a sea-shell.

Papyrus rolls were a considerable improvement over the brick-like cuneiform tablets, but they were not as convenient as the modern book. A papyrus roll could be 50 or even 100 feet in length, and very heavy. One celebrated papyri was 133 feet long and 17 inches thick! Most books consisted of more than one roll.

> "A great book is a great evil."
> —CALLIMACHUS (c. 305–240 B.C.)

The exasperated, and probably exhausted, Callimachus was employed as chief librarian at the famous library of Alexandria in Egypt. If anyone had good reason to complain, it was certainly poor old Callimachus. During his term of office, he took it upon himself to compile a complete catalog of the library's 700,000-odd rolls of papyrus. Entitled "Tables of those who were outstanding in every phase of culture, and their writing," it ran to over 120 rolls of papyrus when completed. As a typical reward for selfless dedication to the spirit of librarianship, Ptolemy II exiled Callimachus to the desert wastes of Upper Egypt.

The standard form of the book continued to be the roll until the coming of Christianity. Papyrus remained in use, but increasingly, rolls were made of parchment or leather. According to folklore, parchment or vellum was invented by Eumenes II of Pergamum, in Asia Minor, after his papyrus supply suddenly and mysteriously dried up. It seems that the Egyptians, who by sheer chance grew the ancient world's entire papyrus crop, also grew jealous. Eumenes' library in Pergamum was second in size and fame to the one in Alexandria and closing fast. The way the crafty Egyptians figured it, no papyrus meant no book production. They figured wrongly of course. Using dried animal skins, book production thrived and the battle of the libraries continued.

Be it papyrus or parchment it was all expensive. Gradually, though, parchment won out. It was much stronger than papyrus, could be written on both sides, and most important, could be scraped clean and reused. In the monasteries of medieval Europe the monks grew into the habit of ripping apart old books, preferably those of a pagan nature, cleaning off the pages and then using them for their own manuscripts. The original texts of these works, called palimpsests, can often be seen through ultraviolet light.

Monk-librarians were known for treating their books harshly. There were many satirical references to the monk and his books.

"The cleanliness of decent hands would be of great benefit to books as well as scholars, if it were not that the itch and pimples are characteristic of the clergy."
— RICHARD DE BURY (1287–1345)

Around the beginning of the Christian Era, books first began to look like books. By A.D. 400, the codex, leaves of parchment or vellum stitched together between covers, had largely taken the place of the roll.

The next innovation in the world of the book was paper. Paper had been used in China for hundreds of years, but did not become common in Europe until the fourteenth century. Of course, there were holdouts.

> "A book on cheap paper does not convince. It
> is not prized, it is like a wheezy doctor with
> ... tobacco breath, who needs a manicure."
> — ELBERT HUBBARD (1856–1915)

The influx of cheap paper meant an increase in the number of books. This did not please everyone. So-called important documents continued to be written on rolls of parchment or even papyrus.

> "Thou hast most traitorously corrupted the youth
> of the realm ... thou hast built a paper mill."
> — WILLIAM SHAKESPEARE (1564–1616)

Codex and paper paved the way for the last and greatest innovation in books — printing. The effect of movable type on the world was electric.

> "'Gracious heavens!' he cries out, leaping up
> and catching hold of his hair, 'What's this?
> Print!'"
> — CHARLES DICKENS (1812–1870)

There were more than a few who did not like this new invention.

> "Books are fatal they are the curse of the
> human race. Nine-tenths of existing books are
> nonsense, and the clever books are the refuta-
> tion of that nonsense. The greatest misfortune
> that ever befell man was the invention of print-
> ing."
> — BENJAMIN DISRAELI (1804–1881)

The first printer in the English language was the merchant William Caxton (1422–1491). The fortunate Caxton had made enough money in trade to devote his last years to literary pursuits. During a stay in Cologne, he learned the art of printing with movable type. In 1474, Caxton set up his own press at Brugge, in Flanders. It was here that he produced the first printed book in the English language. This first book was not, as you might expect, the Bible (at the time, the possession of an English language Bible was seen as evidence of Protestant heresy) but a racy little pot-boiler entitled *Recuyell of the Historyes of Troye,* a fairly typical romance of the period. Shortly thereafter, this was followed by *The Game and Playe of Chesse.* In 1476 Caxton returned to England and set up shop near Westminster Abbey. Within a few months he printed an indulgence and the *Dictes and Sayings of the Philosphres.* During the remainder of his life, Caxton issued almost 100 titles including Chaucer, Malory's *Morte d'Arthur,* and translations of Cicero and *Aesop's Fables.*

Books printed before 1500 are called incunabula, from the Latin word for cradle. About 40,000 such incunabula are preserved in library collections around the world.

> "'How delightful! How wonderful! What a
> privilege to see such treasures! Tell me,' she
> added, turning to the librarian, 'are they *all*
> Caxtons?' This story the observer told later to
> a distinguished American librarian, who lis-
> tened to it attentively, and then said: 'Well,
> were they?'"
> —HELEN HAINES (1872–1961)
> (This anecdote concerns a wealthy lady
> viewing a collection of Shakespeare quar-
> tos. Caxton died seventy-three years be-
> fore the Bard was even born. Of course,
> you knew that.)

Books spread like wildfire. Within fifty years of the invention of printing, there were 9 million printed books in Europe! A single printer could, and did, turn out as many copies of the works of Aristotle in a month as had ever existed.

"Of making many books there is no end."
—Ecclesiastes

But of what value are books? Opinions have differed widely over the centuries.

"Get stewed: books are a load of crap."
—Philip Larkin (1922–1985)

"There's nothing like a heavy book for throwing at noisy cats. And thin books are just the thing to put under shaky tables and chairs. And look at this leather-bound volume. It makes an ideal razorstrop. Books are ideal gifts. I can't get enough of them."
—Mark Twain (1835–1910)

"Quite recently I heard a man say that a wall of books was the best firebreak a house could have because they burn so slowly."
—Robertson Davies (1913–   )

"My books have kept me from the ring, the dog-pit, the tavern and the saloon."
—Thomas Hood (1799–1845)

"For what expectation do you base upon your books that you are always unrolling them and rolling them up, gluing them, trimming them, smearing them with saffron and oil just as if you were going to derive some profit from them?"
—Lucian (c. 180–120 B.C.)

"Few books have more than one thought: the generality indeed have not quite so many."
—Julius Charles Hare (1795–1855) and Augustus William Hare (1792–1834)

"We get our morals from books. I didn't
get mine from books, but I know that
morals come from books — theoretically at
least."
— MARK TWAIN (1835–1910)

"What is responsible for the success of
many works is the rapport between the
mediocrity of the author's ideas and the
mediocrity of the public's."
— NICHOLAS CHAMFORT (1741–1794)

"Books are good enough in their own
way, but they are a mighty bloodless
substitute for life."
— ROBERT LOUIS STEVENSON
(1850–1894)

"Burglars, by the way, never do steal
books; a very significant fact."
— WALTER MURDOCH (1874–1970)

Some people place an undue value on the external appearance of a book.

"Pollio who values nothing that's within,
Buys books as men hunt beavers — for
their skins."
— BENJAMIN FRANKLIN (1706–1790)

"'May I ask you sir, why they are
there?' [A reference to his host's books.]
'To be looked at, sir; just to be looked
at; the reason for most things in a
gentleman's house being in it at all; from
the paper on the walls, and the drapery
of the curtains, even to the books in the
library, of which the most essential part
is the appearance of the back.'"
— THOMAS LOVE PEACOCK (1785–1866)

There are books which deserve this fate.

"There are books of which the backs and
covers are by far the best portion."
— CHARLES DICKENS (1812–1870)

"A servant once asked a London book-
seller for a quantity of printed matter to
fill his master's library shelves. In the first
place I want six feet of theology, the
same quantity of metaphysics, and near a
yard of old civil law, in folio."
— THE ENCYCLOPEDIA OF ANECDOTES
(1884)

Some people have gone to the other extreme, believing that
the content of a book is the only thing which matters.

"Due attention to the inside of books and
due contempt for the outside, is the
proper relation between a man of sense
and his books."
— LORD CHESTERFIELD (1694–1773)

"In some respects the better a book is, the
less it demands from binding . . . such a
book, for instance, as the *Life of the
Duke of Newcastle*, by his Duchess — no
casket is rich enough, no casing sufficiently
durable, to honour and keep safe such a
jewel."
— CHARLES LAMB (1775–1834)

A few scurvy knaves have dared to put a crass monetary
value on books. Booklovers have reacted with justifiable outrage.

"The prices paid for first editions are no real
evidence of the value of a book or the eminence
of the author. Indeed the 'first edition' hobby is
one of the minor forms of mental derangement,
seldom ending in homicide, and outside the scope
of the law."
— STEPHEN LEACOCK (1869–1944)

"There is no special virtue in first editions: one would usually prefer to read a later one in which the printing is up to date, the paper has not faded and the author has corrected the errors. All this trade is as deeply boring to people who are interested in literature as it seems to be fascinating to those others who, incapable of literary culture, try to buy the distinction of letters by paying unusual prices for bibliographical rarities ... it is doubtful whether any first-rate man of letters has ever gone in for collecting books except on some special subject in which he might happen to be interested ... it is easier for a camel to pass through the eye of a needle than for a collector of first editions to enter the Kingdom of Literature."
—EDMUND WILSON (1895–1972)

"How long most people would look at the best book before they would give the price of a large turbot for it."
—JOHN RUSKIN (1819–1900)

Far too many individuals place a value on neither the cover nor its contents.

"Another damned thick square book! Always scribble, scribble, scribble! Eh! Mr. Gibbon."
—WILLIAM HENRY, DUKE OF GLOUCESTER (1743–1805) (Comment made to Edward Gibbon upon being presented with a copy of Gibbon's monumental work, *Decline and Fall of the Roman Empire*.)

Books have been compared to many things. They have been compared to reflections:

"A book is a mirror: If an ass peers into it, you can't expect an apostle to look out."
— GEORG CHRISTOLPH LICTENBERG
(1764–1799)

and to edible tubers:

"Books take their place according to their specific gravity as surely as potatoes in a tub."
— RALPH WALDO EMERSON (1803–1882)

One man compared books to just about everything.

"This genus comprises as its species, gaming, swinging or swaying on a chair or gate; spitting over a bridge; smoking; snuff taking; tete-a-tete quarrels after dinner between husband and wife; conning word for word all the advertisements of the *Daily Advertiser* in a public house on a rainy day, etc. etc. etc."
— SAMUEL TAYLOR COLERIDGE (1772–1834)

Inevitably, books have been compared, by men, to women — and not too kindly.

"Almost any law book that is more than twenty-one years of age, like a single lady who has attained that climacteric, is said to be too old for much devotion."
— HORACE BINNEY (1780–1875)

"One would imagine that books were like women, the worse for being old; that they have a pleasure in being read for the first time; that they open their leaves more cordially; that the spirit of enjoyment wears out with the spirit of novelty; and that, after a certain age, it is high time to put them on the shelf."
— WILLIAM HAZLITT (1778–1830)
(Aside from being sexist, that was close to being pornographic.)

The use one makes of books can reveal much of a person's character.

"It is just those books which a man
possesses, but does not read, which con-
stitute the most suspicious evidence
against him."
    —Victor Hugo (1802–1885)

"When I was a lad I put books inside my
trousers whenever a good spanking was
due me. Ever since I've known the value
of a literary education."
    —Duke Ellington (1899–1974)

One common complaint, usually heard from the unbooked, is that books are time wasters, breeding laziness and sloth.

"The cure for this ill is not to sit still
Or frowst with a book by the fire,
But to take a large hoe and shovel also,
And dig till you gently perspire."
    —Rudyard Kipling (1865–1936)

"Reading all these long-gone-with-the
        winded novels,
Some people are going gaga;
What this country needs is a good five-
        cent saga."
    —David T.W. McCord (1897–   )

The reading of too many books can give rise to certain undesirable effeminacy in their owners.

"For you muddled with books and pictures,
an' china an' etchin's an' fans,
And your rooms at college was beastly—
more like a whore's than a man's."
    —Rudyard Kipling (1865–1936)

Books can cause curious physical defects.

> "Up! up! my Friend, and quit your books;
> Or surely you'll grow double;
> Up! up! my Friend, and clear your looks;
> Why all this toil and trouble?"
> —WILLIAM WORDSWORTH (1770–1850)

We have all smelled a musty book, but some believe the contents of a book can smell bad.

> "Books for all the world are always foul-
> smelling books: the smell of small people
> clings to them."
> —FRIEDRICH NIETZSCHE (1844–1900)

> "Books for general reading always smell
> badly; the odour of common people
> hangs about them. Best-sellers are always
> ill-smellers, sticky with the odour of small
> people."
> —FRIEDRICH NIETZSCHE (1844–1900)
> (Nietzsche seems to be unique in
> history for his obsession with the
> repulsive olfactory qualities of the
> printed word and of its readers.)

But books can be much worse than just foul smelling, they can (horrors!), lead the tender innocent astray.

> "Then Tomlinson he gripped the bars and
> yammered,
> 'Let me in—
> 'For I mind that I borrowed my neigh-
> bour's wife
> to sin the deadly sin.'
> The devil he grinned behind the bars,
> and banked the fires high:
> 'Did ye read of that sin in a book?' said he;
> and Tomlinson said 'Ay!'"
> —RUDYARD KIPLING (1865–1936)

> "Ruined by a book! Such was my awful fate.
> Henry Miller had no effect on me; D.H.
> Lawrence left me cold; I yawned my way
> through Frank Harris's memoirs. But then I
> came across a copy of Eaton's catalogue; and,
> leafing idly through it, discovered photographs
> of men wearing full-length winter undergar-
> ments."
> — RICHARD NEEDHAM (1912–   )

The book disease, if not caught in time, can send the reader straight to perdition.

> "Ugly Hell, gape not! Come not Lucifer! I'll
> burn my books."
> — CHRISTOPHER MARLOWE (1564–1593)

Some books are so dreary as to actively discourage reading.

> "One of those over-annotated editions of a
> book — a book which has so many footnotes
> that the text is crowded right out of bed; a
> book in which the editor is so pleased with
> himself for discovering that the father of Lady
> Hester Somebody . . . was born in 1718 and
> died in 1789, that he simply has not the decent
> manners to keep his useless information to
> himself. No, he must tell it to you, although he
> elbows the author out of the way to do it."
> — EDMUND PEARSON (1880–1937)

Before we leave the subject of books entirely, there are three sub-classes that must be dealt with, the New Book, the Best Seller, and the dreaded Non-Book.
The New Book:

> "What refuge is there for the victim who is op-
> pressed with the feeling that there are a thou-
> sand new books he ought to read, while life is
> only long enough for him to read a hundred."
> — OLIVER WENDELL HOLMES (1809–1894)

"When a new book is published, read an old one."
—SAMUEL ROGERS (1763–1855)

"For reading New Books is like eating new bread;
One can bear it at first but by gradual steps
He is brought to death's door of a mental dyspepy."
—JAMES RUSSELL LOWELL (1819–1891)

"I hate having new books forced upon
me, but how I love cram-throating other
people with them."
—LOGAN PEARSALL SMITH (1865–1946)

The Best Seller:

"The author of the best seller of last week
is thought by the police of repeating his
offense."
—AMBROSE BIERCE (1842–1914?)

"A best seller is the gilded tomb of a
mediocre talent."
—LOGAN PEARSALL SMITH (1865–1946)

The Non-Book:

"I confess it moves my spleen to see these
things in books' clothing perched upon my
shelves. I can read anything which I call a
book. There are things in that shape which I
cannot allow for such. In this catalogue of
*books which are not books—biblia a-biblia—*I
reckon Court Calendars, Directories, Pocket
Books ... and the works of Hume, Gibbon
... and generally all those volumes which 'no
gentleman's library should be without.'"
—CHARLES LAMB (1775–1834)
(At least Lamb did not include books of
quotations.)

As for the future of the book, and the society which nurtures it:

> "This will never be a civilized country until we expend more money for books than we do for chewing gum."
> — ELBERT HUBBARD (1856–1915)

4

Bookworms

"After love, book collecting is the most ex-
hilarating sport of all."
— Abraham Simon Wolf Rosenbach
(1876–1952)

The term bookworm is properly applied to any number of loathsome insects that burrow, nest, feed and breed on dry book paper. The silverfish and the aptly named book-louse are the common varieties.

"Booklice are tiny, pale, wingless insects less than 13mm long. They are yellowish, gray or brownish, with soft bodies and relatively large heads."
— CANADIAN DEPARTMENT OF AGRICULTURE (1977)

"If you find a few booklice in your home, you can probably get rid of them by cleaning your house thoroughly and by sunning, drying and airing the infested rooms."
— CANADIAN DEPARTMENT OF AGRICULTURE (1977)

There is a human type of this curious species as well. How can he or she be recognized?

"He hath not fed of the dainties that are bred in a book; he hath not eat paper, as it were; he hath not drunk ink: his intellect is not replenished; he is only an animal, only sensible in the duller parts."
— WILLIAM SHAKESPEARE (1564–1616)
(Such a person is no bookworm.)

"When I get a little money, I buy books; and if any is left, I buy food and clothes."
— DESIDERUS ERASMUS (c. 1466–1536)
(This person is a bookworm.)

"Yea, he will write books, that he may buy books."
— HENRY WARD BEECHER (1813–1887)
(An extreme form of the disease.)

The bookworm, or bibliophile as he is known in polite company, is always a breed apart.

"A print addict is a man who reads in elevators. People occasionally look at me curiously when they see me standing there, reading a paragraph or two as the elevator goes up. To me, it's curious that there are people who do not read in elevators. What can they be thinking about?"
—ROBERT FULFORD (1932–)

"How easily one may distinguish a genuine lover of books from the worldly man! With what subdued and yet glowing enthusiasm does he gaze upon the costly front of a thousand embattled volumes! How gently he draws them down, as if they were little children; how tenderly he handles them! He peers at the title-page, at the text, or the notes, with the nicety of a bird examining a flower. He studies the binding: the leather, — Russia, English calf, morocco; the lettering, the gilding, the edging, the hinge of the cover! He opens it, and shuts it, he holds it off, and he brings it nigh. It suffuses his whole body with book-magnetism."
—HENRY WARD BEECHER (1813–1887)

"To turn over the pages of a book long coveted, to handle an unexpected find, to fondle a binding, to dust the edges, are exquisite joys in which the hand shares with the eye."
—LOUIS OCTAVE UZANNE (1852–1931)

One of the hallmarks of the human bookworm is his instability.

"What wild desires, what restless torments seize the hapless man, who feels the book-disease!"
—JOHN FERRIAR (1761–1815)

"Speak of the appetite for drink; or of a bon-
vivant's relish for a dinner! What are these
mere animal throes and ragings compared with
those fantasies of taste, of those yearnings of
the imagination, of those insatiable appetites of
intellect, which bewilder a student in a great
book-seller's temptation-hall."
— HENRY WARD BEECHER (1813–1887)

At other times, the bookworm is quiet and full of tender con-
cern — but only for books.

"Does it affect you to find your books
wearing out? I mean literally.... The
mortality of all inanimate things is terri-
ble to me but that of books most of all."
— WILLIAM DEAN HOWELLS
(1837–1920)

"The fate of my books is like the impres-
sion of my face. My acquaintances, so
long as I can remember, have always
said. "Seems to me that you look a little
thinner than when I saw you last."
— RALPH WALDO EMERSON
(1803–1882)

Temptation confronts the bookworm at every turn.

"Where is human nature so weak as in the
bookstore."
— HENRY WARD BEECHER (1813–1887)

"I confess to knowing one or two men
... who, on the plea of being pressed
with business, or because they were going
to a funeral, have passed a bookshop in a
strange town without so much as stepping
inside just to see whether the fellow had
anything!"
— AUGUSTINE BIRRELL (1850–1933)

The bookworm is tortured by his craving for what he cannot have.

"*Ballade of the Unattainable*
The Books I cannot hope to buy,
Their phantoms round me waltz and wheel,
They pass before the dreaming eye,
Ere Sleep the dreaming eye can seal.
A kind of literary reel
They dance; but fair their bindings shine.
Prose cannot tell them what I feel, —
The Books that never can be mine!

There frisk Editions rare and shy,
Morocco clad from head to heel;
Shakespearean quartos; Comedy
As first she flashed from Richard Steele;
And quaint De Foe on Mrs. Veal;
And lord of landing net and line,
Old Izaak with his fishing creel, —
The Books that never can be mine!

Prince, bear a hopeless Bard's appeal;
Reverse the rules of Mine and Thine;
Make it legitimate to steal
The Books that never can be mine!"
— Andrew Lang (1844–1912)

When he falters there is no depth to which the bookworm will not sink to feed his lust.

"Booklovers are thought by unbookish people
to be gentle and unworldly, and perhaps a few
of them are so. But there are others who will
lie and scheme and steal to get books as wildly
and unconsciously as the dope-taker in pursuit
of his drug."
— Robertson Davies (1913–   )

Bookworms, both insect and human, have existed as long as there have been books.

"Twenty-two acknowledged concubines
and a library of sixty-two thousand
volumes, attested the variety of his in-
clinations; and from the productions
which he left behind him, it appears that
the former as well as the latter were
designed for use rather than ostentation."
—EDWARD GIBBON (1737–1794)
(A comment on Gordian the
Younger, a wealthy Roman.)

"For him was levere have at his beddes
heed
Twenty bookes, clad in blak or reed,
Of Aristotle and his philosophye,
Than robes riche, or fithele, or gay
sautrie."
—GEOFFREY CHAUCER (c. 1340–1400)
(levere=rather; fithele=fiddle;
sautrie=harp)

"I know every book of mine by its scent,
and I have but to put my nose between
the pages to be reminded of all sorts of
things."
—GEORGE GISSING (1857–1903)
(Nietzsche take note.)

"It is a library with living rooms attached."
—BERNARD BERENSON (1865–1959)
(Spoken of his house.)

Despite some fearsome odds, I am confident that the bookworm will continue to exist.

"There are still a few of us booklovers around
despite the awful warning of Marshall McLuhan with his TV era and pending farewell to
Gutenberg."
—FRANK DAVIES (1923–   )

Not just anyone can be a bookworm. It takes much more than simply owning a large stock of books. Being a bookworm is an art. Like anything else it has to be cultivated. Benjamin Disraeli, for example, enjoyed watching sunbeams dance on the bindings of his books.

"Much depends upon *when* and where you read a book. In the five or six impatient minutes before the dinner is quite ready, who would think of taking up the Faery Queen for a stop-gap, or a volume of Bishop Andrewes' sermons?"
— CHARLES LAMB (1775–1834)
(For that matter, who would think of taking up the *Faerie Queene* or Bishop Andrewes' sermons in the five or six impatient minutes *after* dinner?)

"All good and true book-lovers practise the pleasing and improving avocation of reading in bed."
— EUGENE FIELD (1850–1895)

"There is a great deal of difference between the eager man who wants to read a book, and the tired man who wants a book to read."
— G.K. CHESTERTON (1874–1936)

Extreme bookworms are literally incapable of doing anything unaided by print.

"A print addict must read all the time, or as close to all the time as makes no difference. He reads at the bus stop, in the bathtub, while the toast is toasting, while the man in the liquor store goes for his liquor. If he drives a car he probably has a little book-holder fastened to his dashboard, so he can read at red lights. He even reads as he walks along the street, sometimes — some percentage of pedestrian traffic accidents can probably be traced directly to print addiction. If a print addict can find nothing else to read he will examine the French on a

breakfast food package, or a subway
transfer, or the advertising on a match-
book. If he stops reading for more than a
few minutes, he grows edgy and begins
looking around for a fix."
    —ROBERT FULFORD (1932–)

       "I may chance, some quiet day, to lay my
       over-beating temples on a book, and so
       have the death I most envy."
          —LEIGH HUNT (1784–1859)

Sometimes the bookworm will attempt to cloak his addiction.

       "I knew a gentleman who was so good a
       manager of his time that he would not even
       lose that small portion of it which the calls of
       nature obliged him to pass in the necessary
       house; but gradually went through all the Latin
       poets in those moments."
          —LORD CHESTERFIELD (1694–1773)

However, take heed all you potential bookworms.

       "Solitary reading is apt to give the headache."
          —CHARLES LAMB (1775–1834)

You can overdo it!

"There are some people who read too
much: the bibliobibuli. I know some who
are constantly drunk on books, as other
men are drunk on whiskey or religion.
They wander through this most diverting
and stimulating of worlds in a haze, see-
ing nothing and hearing nothing."
    —H.L. MENCKEN (1880–1956)

       "When you are speaking of children's
       books it is no idle metaphor to say that
       their owners devoured their contents."
          —GEORGE LESLIE BROOK (1910–)

5

Borrowing and Lending

"I am known as Dr. Jekyll, but I have a dark side,
As the kleptomaniac, bibliomaniac, book purloining
                    Hyde.
My better self as Jekyll, is professionally chaste—
You'd never think to look at me that I was double-faced;
But when I get the urge to handle other people's books
The fingers of the surgeon change to predatory hooks!
As the kindly Dr. Jekyll I am often asked to pick
A volume that I fancy from the bookshelves of the sick;
But once within my bookcase, it is fated to reside
As a permanent addition to the library of Hyde.
It isn't that I can't afford to buy the books I read,
As the wealthy Dr. Jekyll, I can purchase all I need;
But I gaze at my collection—and the devil's half of me
Whispers . . ., 'Such a lot of literature—and all
acquired free!'"
         —P. NICHOLSON

The human species, according to the best
theory I can form of it, is composed of two
distinct races, the men who borrow, and the
men who lend."
— CHARLES LAMB (1775–1834)

Book collections of old were never intended for the masses.
To borrow a book was usually out of the question. The written
word was much too powerful a weapon to be handed out indis-
criminately. In Mesopotamia and Egypt, books were reserved ex-
clusively for the priestly class or nobility. It was not until Greece
and Rome that libraries were started for the use of the public.
Even then the volumes were guarded jealously and never allowed
outside the reading room.

Well, almost never. Certain arrangements could be made for
individuals of sufficient importance. Marcus Aurelius, writing in
A.D. 145, advises a friend not to seek a certain volume at the
Library of Apollo, as he has already signed it out. He tells his
friend to go somewhere else and perhaps bribe a librarian!

In the monasteries of the Middle Ages books were so trea-
sured that they had to be kept in a locked cupboard at night. During the day a monk could only use one book at a time. He could
not take it back to his room and had to use it, under close supervi-
sion, in the library. Interestingly enough, there was a thing called
the intermonastery loan. Monasteries from as far as England and
Greece would borrow from each other. A deposit of money, equal
in value to the book, was required. On at least one occasion the
deposit was lost on account of the book being eaten by a bear! No
word about the borrower. As librarians were held personally
responsible for the loss of any books, very little borrowing oc-
curred. The heavily used books were chained in place.

"The laity, who look at a book turned upside
down just as if it were open in the correct way
are utterly unworthy of any communion with
books."
— RICHARD DE BURY (1287–1345)

The most liberal lending policies were in the great libraries of the Islamic world. Undoubtedly, this was due to their relatively vast fund of books. A thirteenth century Islamic scholar reported that he was able to keep two hundred volumes in his room at one time. Two hundred volumes equaled the entire collection of most European libraries.

The early universities were not much better than the monasteries. At the Sorbonne, in the fourteenth century, every borrowed book had to be returned before sundown. Outsiders, even the nobility, had to leave a hefty deposit, or a book of equal value. The New College Library at Oxford was amazingly liberal. Each fellow of the college was given his own key to the library and allowed to borrow a remarkable two books at one time, and keep them for up to a year! Reference books, however, were chained firmly in place, and a yearly inventory was taken of the holdings.

In most places, rather than trying to bring the book and the reader together, the emphasis was on keeping the book and reader apart. This was never more true than when the reader was a student.

> "The handling of books is specially to be forbidden to those shameless youths, who as soon as they have learned to form the shapes of letters, straightaway, if they have the opportunity become unhappy commentators, and wherever they find an extra margin about the text, furnish it with monstrous alphabets, or if any other frivolity strikes their fancy, at once their pen begins to write it. There the Latinist and sophister and every unlearned writer tries the fitness of his pen, a practice that we have frequently seen injuring the usefulness and value of the most beautiful books."
> —Richard de Bury (1287–1345)

There were volumes in university libraries kept under triple lock. The key to each lock was held by a different person. All three had to be present before the intimidated student could use the book. As late as 1850 some American college libraries were open a grand total of one hour every two weeks!

The librarian, as we have seen, was merely pitied. The book borrower, in contrast, was, and largely still is, *despised*. This is a universal truth, be he patron of the public library or ravisher of the private collection.

> "Great collections of books are subject to certain accidents besides the damp, the worms, and the rats; one not less common is that of the *borrowers*, not to say a word of the *purloiners*."
> —Isaac D'Israeli (1766–1848)

No one has a kind word to say for this creature known as the book borrower. Take note of this description from the fourteenth century.

> "You may happen to see some headstrong youth lazily lounging over his studies, and when the winter's frost is sharp, his nose running from the nipping cold drips down, nor does he think of wiping it with his pocket-handkerchief until he has bedewed the book before him with the ugly moisture. Would that he had before him no book but a cobbler's apron!
> "His nails are stuffed with fetid filth as black as jet, with which he marks any passage that pleases him. He distributed a multitude of straws, which he inserts to stick out in different places, so that the halm may remind him of what his memory cannot retain. These straws, because the book has no stomach to digest them, and no one takes them out, first distend the book from its wonted closing, and at length, being carelessly abandoned to oblivion, go to decay.
> "He does not fear to eat fruit or cheese over an open book, or to carelessly carry a cup to and from his mouth; and because he has no wallet at hand he drops into books the

fragments that are left. Continually chattering,
he is never weary of disputing with his compa-
nions, and while he alleges a crowd of senseless
arguments, he wets the book lying half open
on his lap with sputtering showers. Aye, and
then hastily folding his arms he leans forward
on the book, and by a brief spell of study in-
vites a prolonged nap; and then, by way of
mending the wrinkles, he folds back the margin
of the leaves, to the no small injury of the
book.

"Now the rain is over and gone, and the
flowers have appeared in our land. Then the
scholar we are speaking of, a neglector rather
than an inspector of books, will stuff his
volume with violets, and primroses, with roses
and quatrefoil. Then he will use his wet and
perspiring hands to turn over the volumes;
then he will thump the white vellum with
gloves covered with all kinds of dust, and with
his finger clad in long-used leather will hunt
line by line through the page; then at the sting
of the biting flea the sacred book is flung aside,
and is hardly shut for another month, until it is
so full of the dust that has found its way
within, that it resists the effort to close it."

— RICHARD DE BURY (1287–1345)

Medieval monks were driven to pen curses against this des-
picable species.

"The lending books, as well as the smaller
without pictures, as the larger with pictures, is
forbidden under the penalty of excommunica-
tion."

— INGULF, ABBOT OF CROYLAND (d. 1109)

Even popes felt threatened by the book borrower.

"Whoever writes his name here in acknowledgment of books received on loan out of the
Pope's Library, will incur his anger and his
curse unless he return them uninjured within a
very brief period."
　　　—Pope Nicholas V (c. 1397–1455)

To the bibliophile there can be nothing worse than a book
thief.

"Next o'er his books his eyes began to
roll, in pleasing memory of all he stole."
　　　—Alexander Pope (1688–1744)

"Steal not this book, for fear of shame,
For it is in the owner's name;
And when you're dead, the Lord will say,
'Where is that book you stole away?'"
　　　—Anon. (Book inscription.)

Hanging was too good for such persons.

"Steal not this book, my honest friend,
For fear the gallows be thine end."
　　　—Anon. (Book inscription.)

The problem is that the book borrower is probably a bibliophile just like the book lender.

"Never lend books—nobody ever returns them,
the only books I have in my library are those
which people have lent me."
　　　—Anatole France (1844–1924)

If someone willingly lends you a book it is a sure sign that
it is yours in the first place.

"Knowing I lov'd my books, he furnish'd me,
From mine own library with volumes that
I prize above my dukedom."
—WILLIAM SHAKESPEARE (1564–1616)

Over the years there has been a steady stream of advice, indeed warning, from those who have been borrowed from. It ranges from the terse...

"Borrow from yourself."
—CATO THE ELDER (234–149 B.C.)

"He that lends gives."
—GEORGE HERBERT (1593–1633)

... to the jocular.

"He that lendeth to all that will borrow,
sheweth great good will, but little wit."
—JOHN LYLY (c. 1554–1606)

"Hard-covered books break up friendships. You loan a hard-covered book to a friend and when he doesn't return it you get mad at him. It makes you mean and petty. But 25¢ books are different."
—JOHN STEINBECK (1902–1968)
(When is the last time you saw a book for a quarter?)

"Everything comes to him who waits but a loaned book."
—Frank McKinney "Kin" Hubbard (1868–1930)

"Such is the fate of borrowed books:
they're lost,
Or not the book returneth, but its ghost!"
—ANDREW LANG (1844–1912)

The message is clear.

"Lend only what you can afford to lose."
— GEORGE HERBERT (1593–1633)

The more of these statements you read you notice how many of them have an aura of bitterness and despair about them. Book borrowers are everywhere and there is no effective defense.

"A person's library consists of all the books he has that no one wants to borrow."
— ANON.

"Friends: People who borrow my books and set wet glasses on them."
— EDWARD ARLINGTON ROBINSON (1869–1935)

"Please return this book; I find that though many of my friends are poor arithmeticians, they are nearly all good bookkeepers."
— SIR WALTER SCOTT (1771–1832)

"They borrow books they will not buy, They have no ethics or religions, I wish some kind Burbankian guy Could cross my books with homing pigeons."
— CAROLYN WELLS (1869–1942)

Borrowed books are missing books. They spoil the sense of completeness so dear to the confirmed bibliophile's heart.

"Which of our shelves is safe?"
— CHARLES LAMB (1775–1834)

Charles Lamb, poet, critic and co-author, with his sister Mary, of *Tales from Shakespeare*, felt the searing sting of the lost book more acutely than most.

"That foul gap in the bottom shelf facing
you, like a great eye-tooth knocked out.
"The slight vacuum in the left-hand case —
two shelves from the ceiling. . . . In yonder
nook . . . a widower-volume . . . mourns his
ravished mate.
"Reader, if haply thou art blest with a
moderate collection, be shy of showing it; or if
thy heart overfloweth to lend them, lend thy
books; but lend them not to such a one as
S.T.C. — he will return them with usury; en-
riched with annotations tripling their value. I
have had experience. Many of these precious
MSS. of his — (in *matter* oftentimes, and almost
in *quantity* not unfrequently, vying with the
originals) and in no very clerky hand . . . I
counsel thee, shut not thy heart, nor thy
library, against S.T.C."
　　　— CHARLES LAMB (1775–1834)
　　　(S.T.C. — Samuel Taylor Coleridge)

Among the worst victims of the book borrower is the librarian.

"To maintain a public library intact, the librarian should buy
three copies of each book: the first to show, the second to loan
and the third to read."
　　— ANON.

"One whole side of an immense store is not only
filled with most admirably bound library-books, but
from some inexhaustible source the void continually
made in the shelves is at once refilled."
　　— HENRY WARD BEECHER (1813–1887)

"Gilt edges, vellum and morocco, and
presentation copies to all the libraries will
not preserve a book in circulation."
　　— RALPH WALDO EMERSON
　　(1803–1882)

Of course the librarian gets no respect.

> "Out of my lean and low ability
> I'll lend you something."
> —WILLIAM SHAKESPEARE (1564–1616)

One book borrower, who wisely chose to protect his anonymity, to say nothing of his life, actually dared to complain about the circulation service.

> "The only source from which you can't keep
> books that you have borrowed is the public
> library."
> —ANON.

Last, we must make mention of the worst pest of all, the reverse book borrower—the book giver.

> "The books we think we ought to read are
> poky, dull and dry;
> The books we would like to read we are
> ashamed to buy
> The books that people talk about we never can
> recall;
> And the books that people give us, oh they're
> the worst of all."
> —CAROLYN WELLS (1869–1942)

6

Censorship

"Some books, like the City of London, fare
the better for being burned."
  — THOMAS BROWN (1663–1704)

Call it magic and superstition, government regulation, or religious edict, there has probably never been a society free from censorship.

> "Those books are condemned which are derog-
> atory to God, or the Virgin Mary, or the
> Saints, or the Catholic Church and her wor-
> ship, or to the Sacraments or the Holy See. So
> also are condemned those books in which the
> idea of the inspiration of Holy Scripture is
> perverted. So also are condemned those books
> which revile the ecclesiastical hierarchy or the
> clerical or religious state."
> — POPE LEO XIII (1810–1903)

It is not entirely without significance that the first "keepers of books" in ancient Mesopotamia were also censors of books. "Inspector of Scribes" was a typical title. Since those days there has always been someone somewhere who wants to ban a book because of its alleged subversive, or morally corrupting, qualities.

> "Damn all expurgated books; the dirtiest
> book of all is the expurgated book."
> — WALT WHITMAN (1819–1882)

> "A censor is a man who knows more than
> he thinks you ought to know."
> — LAURENCE J. PETER (1919–1990)

Augustus, who founded the first public library in Rome, took a profound dislike to the poet Ovid. He had Ovid's works removed from the library, and Ovid himself removed to the outer reaches of the Black Sea. Ovid's unhappy fate may have had something to do with the poet's pioneering work of sex instruction, *Ars Amatoria* or *Art of Love*, a three volume book once described as being, just possibly, the most depraved work ever conceived by the mind of a genius. The list of "dirty" and objectionable books is a long one, including titles like *Lady Chatterley's Lover, Fanny Hill, Tropic of Capricorn, Ulysses,* and anything by

the Marquis de Sade. *Huckleberry Finn* always finds a place on
this exalted list.

> "If there is an Unexpurgated in the Children's
> Department won't you please help that young
> woman remove Huck from that questionable
> companionship."
> —MARK TWAIN (1835–1910)
> (By Unexpurgated, Twain is referring to
> the Bible.)

A few people flatly deny that offensive books exist.

> "There is no such thing as a moral or an im-
> moral work. Books are well written or badly
> written. That is all."
> —OSCAR WILDE (1854–1900)

The printing press proved to be the censor's greatest chal-
lenge. As far as the forces of law and decency were concerned,
much of the vast outpouring of printed literature was morally im-
pure or seditious. It had to be stopped!

> "The new invention of printing has pro-
> duced various effects of which your
> Holiness cannot be ignorant. If it has
> restored books and learning, it has also
> been the occasion of those sects and
> schisms which appear daily. Men begin to
> call in question the present faith and
> tenets of the Church; the laity read the
> Scripture and pray in the vulgar
> tongue. . . . The mysteries of religion must
> be kept in the hands of priests."
> —CARDINAL WOLSEY (1475–1530)

> "The multitude of books is a great evil.
> There is no measure or limit to this fever
> of writing; everyone must be an author;
> some out of vanity to acquire celebrity;
> others for the sake of lucre and gain."
> —MARTIN LUTHER (1483–1546)

In an effort to control the traffic in printed matter a rigid censorship was established in most countries.

> "Books are not good fuel ... In the days when
> heretical books were burned, it was necessary
> to place them on large wooden stages, and
> after all the pains taken to demolish them, considerable readable masses were sometimes
> found in the embers; whence it was supposed
> that the devil, conversant in fire and its effects,
> gave them his special protection. In the end it
> was found easier and cheaper to burn the heretics themselves than their books."
> —JOHN HILL BURTON (1809–1881)

In England the Stationers' Company was formed; so named because they were permitted to set up bookshops in one place and not have to keep moving to avoid the arm of the law. No book, pamphlet or news sheet could be printed without a license from the Stationers—the Bible included. Licensors were appointed to read books and decide if they were heretical, obscene, libelous, or politically unacceptable. As a further control, the number of master printers was limited to twenty. Not surprisingly, a large book smuggling industry sprang up almost immediately.

Stationers were popular with no one.

> "If I were to paint sloth ... by St. John the
> Evangelist I swear, I would draw it like a Stationer that I know, with his thumb under his
> girdle, who if a man comes to his stall and ask
> him for a book, never stirs his head, or looks
> upon him, but stands stone still, and speaks
> not a word: only, with his little finger points
> backwards to his boy, who must be his interpreter and so all the day, gaping like a dumb
> image, he sits without motion."
> —THOMAS NASHE (1567–1601)

Those who patronized the stationers were not popular either.

"Ignorant asses visiting stationer's shops their use is not to inquire for good books but for new ones."
— JOHN WEBSTER (1580–1625)

The stationers exercised their tyranny until licensing was eliminated by an Act of Parliament in 1625. Of course there are still those who feel the need to censor books.

"A writer owned an asterisk,
And kept it in his den,
Where he wrote tales (which had large
                              sales)
Of frail and erring men;
And always, when he reached the point
Where carping censors lurk,
He called upon the asterisk
To do his dirty work."
— STODDARD KING (1890–1933)

"I wonder why murder is considered less immoral than fornication in literature?"
— GEORGE MOORE (1852–1933)

"There is so much nastiness in modern literature that I like to write stories which contain nothing more than a little innocent murdering."
— EDGAR WALLACE (1875–1932)

"Perhaps I have hit on a reason for my waning love of novels which I was not aware — that they have substituted gynaecology for romance."
— BEN HECHT (1894–1964)

"Was ever a book containing such vile matter so fairly bound?"
— WILLIAM SHAKESPEARE (1564–1616)

"Both Catholic and Anglican hold the city by
the throat, and mould the habits and opinions
of the people of Toronto. No book or lecture
can have any success that does not have the
stamp of approval of the churches. Perhaps
you will understand the whole situation when I
tell you that the librarian of the public library
. . . declared: 'No, we do not censor books, we
simply do not get them.' He certainly spoke the
truth."
—EMMA GOLDMAN (1860–1940)

Whenever anything is censored it immediately becomes popular. One of humankind's basic traits is the desire to own a book which must be kept hidden.

"Books being once called in and forbidden
become more saleable and public."
—MICHEL DE MONTAIGNE (1533–1592)

"Chin Shengt'an regards reading a banned
book behind closed doors on a snowy
night as one of the greatest pleasures of
life."
—LIN YUTANG (1895–1976)
(Chin Shengt'an was a seventeenth
century Chinese philosopher. Some
of his other pleasures included light-
ing firecrackers while drunk, open-
ing windows for wasps, and bathing
the eczema spots on his private
parts!)

The most effective way to suppress a book is to ignore it. After all . . .

"Literary sex, unlike literary love is a poor
substitute for the real thing."
—MIRIAM WADDINGTON (1917–   )

7

Classics

"This author has got it made;
No vestige of doubt now lurks
For consider this accolade:
His books are known as works."
— GEORGIE STARBUCK GALBRAITH
(1909–1980)

It is difficult to pinpoint exactly what quality it is that makes a book a classic.

"Another odd thing about classics is that when their authors are writing them, they don't know what they are doing."
— Clifton Fadiman (1904–   )

One thing for sure, you cannot ask the authors; they have a habit of being dead. At the time of writing, a so-called classic resembled what most people read today.

"The whole pleasure of which book standeth in two special points, in open manslaughter and bold bawdy."
— Roger Ascham (1515–1568)
(Spoken about *Le Morte d'Arthur*.)

The first thing we can be certain about is age. In order to be called a classic it helps a book to be old. Even better to be old and Greek.

"An ancient friend of mine, a clergyman, tells me that in Hesiod he finds a peculiar grace that he doesn't find elsewhere. He's a liar."
— Stephen Leacock (1869–1944)

"My friend the professor of Greek tells me that he truly believes that the classics made him what he is. This is a very grave statement; if well founded."
— Stephen Leacock (1869–1944)

A liberal dose of boredom is an essential ingredient in any classic.

"I can see land!"
—Diogenes (c. 412 b.c.–323 b.c.)
(Spoken upon nearing the end of a long
dry book, written by one of his contem-
poraries. Today, without doubt, that
book would be considered a classic.)

With a masochism made perverse by its insistence, the
reading public for classics actually demands that it be bored!

"Make him laugh and he will think you a
trivial fellow, but bore him in the right way
and your reputation is assured."
—William Somerset Maugham
(1874–1965)

The inability to spell can indicate the presence of a writer of
classics.

"It is a pity that Chaucer, who had geneyus,
was so uneducated; he's the wuss speller I
know of."
—Artemus Ward (1834–1867)

Most important of all, any book that aims to be a classic has
to gather dust.

"Books are always the better for not being
read. Look at our classics."
—George Bernard Shaw
(1856–1950)

"'Classic.' A book which people praise
and don't read."
—Mark Twain (1835–1910)

A classic should be treated like any other book. Consider this
sensible advice:

"Give me a book for use! If the margins are too
wide cut them down; if the covers are too
clumsy, tear them off. If you buy a book as a
work of art, put it in your cabinet and order a
modern edition for reading."
— SIR WILLIAM VAN HORNE (1843–1915)

To sum up:

"A work of art? It has no invention; it has no order, system,
sequence, or result; it has no lifelikeness, no thrill, no stir, no
seeming of reality; its characters are confusingly drawn and by
their acts and words they prove they are not the sort of people
the author claims that they are; its humor is pathetic; its pathos
is funny; its conversations — oh! indescribable: its love-scenes
odious, its English a crime against the language. Counting these
out, what is left is Art. I think we must admire that."
— MARK TWAIN (1835–1910)
(Twain is referring to James Fenimore Cooper's classic
novel *The Deerslayer*.)

"Why need to compose a classic for the ages? Why
try so hard to make yourself known to posterity?
You were born to die, and a quiet funeral is less of a
nuisance."
— SENECA (c. 4 B.C.–A.D. 65)

"I will say one further thing about the
classics. *There are not going to be any
more.*"
— STEPHEN LEACOCK (1869–1944)

8

Reading

"What do you read my Lord?"
"Words, words, words."
—WILLIAM SHAKESPEARE (1564–1616)

"No, Sir, do you read books through?"
—SAMUEL JOHNSON (1709–1784)

"Never read a book squire: always think
for yourself."
—THOMAS CHANDLER HALIBURTON
(1796–1865)

Reading is an ancient art. In the form of cuneiform tablets and hieroglyphics it has been around for at least 6,000 years. Yet throughout that long history, apart from a few priests, a few nobles and an occasional educated slave, very few men, and fewer women, were literate or given the chance to become so. Even today, one third of the world's population is illiterate and the rate of functional illiteracy in many of the "advanced" countries is a disgrace. During most of history the ability to read and write has been carefully guarded. The reason was simple: the written word is powerful.

"To pass from hearing literature to reading it is
to take a great and dangerous step."
—ROBERT LOUIS STEVENSON (1850–1894)

Kings could be illiterate, and often were. Charlemagne, ruler of a vast empire, could not read a word though he founded schools throughout his domain. Charlemagne carried around a wax slate and stylus in the hope that he could find the time to learn to read. He never did.

A few people have a natural aptitude for reading.

"I can remember no time at which a page of
print was not intelligible to me, and can only
suppose that I was born literate."
—GEORGE BERNARD SHAW (1856–1950)

Such individuals are rare. Henry I, of England, earned the nickname "Beau-Clerc" simply because he could read. The barons of Magna Carta fame signed with their seals, not with their signatures.

Throughout the Middle Ages what little education there was came from the monasteries. Theology, reading and a little general knowledge were imparted to the sons of the nobles. Only on rare occasions were the promising offspring of the poor included. Yet considerable numbers of people did learn to read. The complexities of trade in the new urban centers made such development a necessity. By the end of the fourteenth century, church registers were beginning to record the existence of a queer new class: the literate layman. A hundred years later this term was no longer in use as the species to which it referred was too common to deserve special mention. The middle class had obtained the wherewithal and the desire to own and read books. Books were becoming cheaper and more numerous.

> "Give me a small snug place almost entirely
> walled with books."
> — LEIGH HUNT (1784–1859)

With this increase in popular literacy came a snobbery, still in existence, associated with "good" reading as opposed to the other variety.

> "I was never allowed to read the popular
> American children's books of my day, as
> my mother said the children spoke bad
> English *without the author's knowing it.*
> — EDITH WHARTON (1862–1937)

> "I know of no sentence that can induce
> such immediate and brazen lying as the
> one that begins, 'Have you read — .'"
> — WILSON MIZNER (1876–1933)

By the nineteenth century, reading had become popular among the lower classes. Needless to say, bibliophiles have usually been contemptuous of what the common folk read.

> "Readers of books, I mean worth-while readers,
> like those who read this volume."
> — STEPHEN LEACOCK (1869–1944)

"Behold her now! She on her sofa looks
O'er half a shelf of circulating books:
This she admired, but she forgets the
        name.
And reads again another, or the same.
She likes to read of strange and bold
        escapes,
Of plans and plottings, murders and
        mishaps,
Love in all hearts, and lovers in all shapes.
She sighs for pity, and her sorrows flow
From the dark eyelash on the page below;
And is so glad when, all the misery past,
The dear adventurous lovers meet at last —
Meet and are happy; and she thinks it
        hard,
When thus an author might a pain
        reward —
When they, the troubles all dispersed,
        might wed —
He makes them part and die of grief
        instead."
    — GEORGE CRABBE (1754–1832)

"On another small table stood Zuleika's
library. Both books were in covers of dull
gold."
    — MAX BEERBOHM (1872–1956)

"Call it rather a sort of beggerly day-
dreaming during which the mind of the
dreamer furnishes for itself nothing but
laziness and a little mawkish sensibility
. . . we should therefore transfer this
species of amusement . . . from the genus,
reading, to that comprehensive class . . .
namely indulgence of sloth and hatred of
vacancy."
    — SAMUEL TAYLOR COLERIDGE
    (1772–1834)

"Guanoed her mind by reading French novels."
— BENJAMIN DISRAELI (1804–1881)

"They're on'ly three books in th' wurruld worth
readin'—Shakespeare, th' Bible, an' Mike Ahearn's
histhry iv Chicago."
— FINLEY PETER DUNNE (1867–1936)

"Hugo, Huxley, Darwin, too,
And twenty score beside,
They lined his book-shelves while he read
'Proud Poll, the Pirate's Bride.'"
— WILBUR DICK NESBIT (1871–1927)

Beside condemning their reading tastes, the "quality" reader
disapproves of the common folk precisely because they do read.

"Occasionally they even wallow in books as
though in their own excrement."
— FRIEDRICH NIETZSCHE (1844–1900)

Then again, the bibliophile and his reading have come in for
their own well-deserved share of criticism.

"The 'bookman' sunk deep in his leather chair
before the fire, his feet in old and comfortable
slippers, his friendly briar filled with the
fragrant Nostalgia Mixture, and a cherished
volume (for 'bookmen' are great cherishers of
volumes and never seem to read one which is
not 'well worn') rises sickeningly before the
eye. A pox, yea, a gleety imposthume upon all
these bookmen and their snug rituals! They
make the whole idea of reading nauseous to
thousands of decent people."
— ROBERTSON DAVIES (1913–   )

It is not often that a serious book lover will admit to reading
popular works.

"I do not remember a more whimsical surprise than having been once detected— by a familiar damsel—reclined at my ease upon the grass, on Primrose Hill, read-ing—*Pamela*. There was nothing in the book to make a man seriously ashamed at the exposure; but as she seated herself down by me, and seemed determined to read in company, I could have wished it had been—any other book. We read on very sociably for a few pages; and not finding the author much to her taste, she got up, and—went away. Gentle casuist, I leave it to thee to conjecture, whether the blush (for there was one between us) was the property of the nymph or the swain in this dilemma."
— CHARLES LAMB (1775–1834)
(*Pamela* [1740], by Samuel Richard-son, is a story of a serving woman who works for a lusty gentleman. It was regarded as a "woman's novel" and quite a racy one. It inspired Henry Fielding's parody, *Shamela*. *Pamela* is now thought of as the first great English novel.)

"Readers can be placed into four classes:
— Sponges, who absorb all they read and return it nearly in the same state, only a little dirtied.
— Sand-glasses, who retain nothing and are content to get through a book for the sake of getting through the time.
— Strain-bags, who retain merely dregs of what they read.
— Mogul diamonds, equally rare and val-uable, who profit by what they read, and enable others to profit by it also."
— SAMUEL TAYLOR COLERIDGE (1772–1834)

The honest reader is one who reads junk and does not care who knows it.

"She looked at the rows of new books, 'Have you anything really shocking...? I adore mucky books and you never have any in stock.'"
— JOHN BRAINE (1922–1986)

What good is reading anyway?

"'What is the use of a book,' thought Alice, 'without pictures or conversations?'"
— LEWIS CARROLL (1832–1898)

"The present craving of adults for picture books makes me wonder if all this past business of reading type-matter has perhaps been a pose."
— ROBERT BENCHLEY (1889–1945)

"Sartor Resartus is simply unreadable, and for me that always sort of spoils a book."
— WILL CUPPY (1864–1949)
(Sartor Resartus, subtitled The Life and Opinions of Herr Teufelsdrockh, by Thomas Carlyle, is concerned with the false dogma of scientific materialism and the sacrament of work, among other things. It is as unreadable a book as you may ever hope to find.)

"I would sooner read a time-table or a catalogue than nothing at all. They are much more entertaining than half the novels that are written."
— WILLIAM SOMERSET MAUGHAM (1874–1965)

The use of reading? It passes the time.

> "I had an exciting day ... reading the statutes
> and the dictionary and wondering how the
> characters would turn out."
> —MARK TWAIN (1835–1910)
> (While on his way to Nevada, by stage
> coach, Twain had nothing to read but the
> dictionary and the legal code.)

It is not just that reading passes the time but that it can do
so in an approved manner.

> "Reading to most people, means an ashamed
> way of killing time disguised under a dignified
> name."
> —ERNEST DIMNET (1866–1954)

Reading further has some value for preventing mental fa-
tigue.

> "Reading is sometimes an ingenious device for
> avoiding thought."
> —SIR ARTHUR HELPS (1813–1875)

It can put you to sleep and wake you up.

> "I fell asleep reading a dull book, and I dreamed
> that I was reading on, so I awoke from sheer
> boredom."
> —HEINRICH HEINE (1797–1856)

Reading can teach you useful things, such as geography . . .

> "There is a work in several volumes in our Cir-
> culating Library entitled Little Reading, which I
> thought referred to a town of that name which
> I had not been to."
> —HENRY DAVID THOREAU (1817–1862)

... or earth science.

> "The Tasmanian Parliamentary Library for sev-
> eral years included in its Geology Section *King
> Solomon's Mines.*"
> —WALTER MURDOCH (1874–1970)

At all costs avoid reading too much. Those who indulge this vice are looked upon with disfavor by almost everyone.

> "A reading-machine, always wound up and
> going,
> He mastered whatever was not worth know-
> ing."
> —JAMES RUSSELL LOWELL (1819–1891)

To get the most out of reading, one has to cultivate the correct technique.

> "The art of reading is to skip judiciously."
> —PHILIP HAMERTON (1834–1894)

> "There was an Old Person of Cromer,
> Who stood on one leg to read Homer,
> When he found he grew stiff, he jumped
> over a cliff,
> Which concluded that person of Cromer."
> —EDWARD LEAR (1812–1888)

Perhaps the luckiest person is the one who does not have to read at all.

> "When I want to read a novel I write one."
> —BENJAMIN DISRAELI (1804–1881)

9

Writing

"Royalties are nice and all but shaking the
beads brings in money quicker."
— GYPSY ROSE LEE (1919–1970)

"The last thing we discover in writing a book,
is what to put at the beginning."
— BLAISE PASCAL (1623–1662)

Why is it that a few otherwise sane individuals want to write?
What demon possesses them?

"No wan iver wrote anythin' because he was
tol' that a hundherd years fr'm now his books
might be taken down fr'm a shelf in a granite
sepulcher an' some wan wud write 'Good' or
'This man is crazy' in the margin."
— FINLEY PETER DUNNE (1867–1936)

Writing is anything but fun.

"Writing a book is a horrible exhausting
struggle, like a long bout of some painful
illness."
— GEORGE ORWELL (1903–1950)

"Writing a book is an adventure, to begin
with it is a toy and an amusement, then it
becomes a master, and then it becomes a
tyrant; and the last phase is just as you
are about to be reconciled to your servi-
tude — you kill the monster and fling him
. . . to the public."
— SIR WINSTON CHURCHILL
(1874–1965)

It is hard on the ego.

"Being a writer in a library is like being a eunuch in
a harem."
— JOHN BRAINE (1922–1986)
(The old eunuch/harem thing again.)

The only praise a writer gets for his labors is that which he
gives himself.

"Good God! What a genius I had when I
wrote that book."
     —JONATHAN SWIFT (1667–1745)

          "I have a library of nearly nine hundred
          volumes, over seven hundred of which I
          wrote myself."
              —HENRY DAVID THOREAU (1817–1862)

There has to be some good reason why people want to write.

     "On the day when a young writer corrects his
     first proof-sheet he is as proud as a schoolboy
     who has just gotten his first dose of the pox."
        —CHARLES BAUDELAIRE (1821–1867)

Surely, desire for fame cannot be the full explanation.

"No man but a blockhead ever wrote except for the money."
     —SAMUEL JOHNSON (1709–1784)

          "The only sensible ends of literature are
          first, the pleasurable toil of writing; sec-
          ond, the gratification of one's family and
          friends; and lastly, the solid cash."
            —NATHANIEL HAWTHORNE (1804–1864)

But it has never been easy to obtain "solid cash" through the
craft of writing.

     "Literature happens to be the only occupation
     in which wages are not given in proportion to
     the goodness of the work done."
        —JAMES FROUDE (1818–1894)

In order to make a living wage a writer will probably have
to surrender his artistic pretensions.

"Literature was formerly an art and finance a trade. Today it is the reverse."
— James Roux (1834–1892)

"If you want to get rich from writing, write the sort of thing that's read by persons who move their lips when they're reading to themselves."
— Don Marquis (1878–1937)

"The life of the writing man has always been ... a bitter business. It is notoriously accompanied for those who write well, by poverty and contempt; or by fatuity and wealth for those who write ill."
— Hillaire Belloc (1870–1953)

No wonder writing has been so often maligned.

"If *Hamlet* had been written these days it would probably have been called *The Strange Affair at Elsinore*."
— Sir James Barrie (1860–1937)

"Most [books] of the present day look as if they had taken a day to write, with the help of books that it had taken a day to read."
— Nicholas Chamfort (1741–1794)

"The naturalistic literature of this country has reached such a state that no family of characters is considered true to life which does not include at least two hypochondriacs, one sadist, and an old man who spills food down the front of his vest."
— Robert Benchley (1889–1945)

"There is no doubt that in many modern novels you get 'a feeling' for things. You get a feeling for old Southern pappies soaking the blood off their knuckles."
— Robert Benchley (1889–1945)

"His instinctive inclination to depict
demented persons, criminals, prostitutes,
and semi-maniacs ... his symbolism, his
pessimism, his coprolalia, and his predi-
lection for slang, sufficiently characterize
M. Zola as a high-class degenerate. That
he is a sexual psychopath is betrayed on
every page of his novels.... His con-
sciousness is peopled with images of un-
natural vice, bestiality, passivism and
other aberrations.... Every porter of a
brothel is capable of relating a low de-
bauch."
  —MAX NORDAU (1849-1923)
  (A very personal opinion about the
  works of Émile Zola.)

"I wonder whether what we are publishing now is worth cutting down trees to
make paper for the stuff."
  —RICHARD BRAUTIGAN (1935-1984)

"Sometimes I think life is much too
serious for fooling around with mere literature."
  —LOUIS DUDEK (1918-)

"Literature is printed nonsense."
  —AUGUST STRINDBERG (1849-1912)

"It took me fifteen years to discover that I
had no talent for writing, but I couldn't
give it up because by that time I was too
famous."
  —ROBERT BENCHLEY (1889-1945)

If you are still interested in being a writer the technique used
in the writing process varies.

"I get up in the morning, torture a typewriter until it screams, then stop."
— CLARENCE BUDINGTON KELLAND (1881–1964)

"The great Sung scholar, Ouyang Hsiu, confessed to 'three on's' for doing his best writing: on the pillow, on horseback and on the toilet."
— LIN YUTANG (1895–1976)

"Never pursue literature as a trade."
— SAMUEL TAYLOR COLERIDGE (1772–1834)

10

Education

"For a well rounded education, you could
try curling up with good books and bad
librarians."
— RICHARD NEEDHAM (1912–   )

"Much study is a weariness for the flesh."
— ECCLESIASTES

Institutions of education have been with us since the invention of the book. During that time, schools have inflicted more than their allotment of misery.

"There is on the whole, nothing on earth intended for innocent people so horrible as a school. To begin with it is a prison. But it is in some respects more cruel than a prison. In a prison, for instance, you are not forced to read books written by the warders and the governor."
— GEORGE BERNARD SHAW (1856–1950)

We must feel pity for the poor inmates.

"The whining school-boy, with his satchel and shining morning face, creeping like a snail unwillingly to school."
— WILLIAM SHAKESPEARE (1564–1616)

"The schoolboy, with his satchel in his hand, whistling aloud to bear his courage up."
— ROBERT BLAIR (1699–1746)

"Hard students are commonly troubled with gowts, catarrhes, rheums, cachexia, bradypepsia, bad eyes, stone, and collick, crudities, oppilations, vertigo, winds, consumptions, and all such diseases as come by overmuch sitting; they are most part time lean, dry, ill-coloured; spend their fortunes, lose their wits, and many times their lives; and all through immoderate pains and extraordinary studies."
— ROBERT BURTON (1577–1640)
(Cachexia=a general state of bad health characterized by a waxy complexion; Bradypepsia=chronic slowness of digestion.)

The stated function of mass education is to enlighten the ignorant.

> "'Reeling and Writhing, of course, to begin
> with,' the Mock Turtle replied, 'and the
> different branches of Arithmetic — Ambition,
> Distraction, Uglification, and Derision.'"
> — LEWIS CARROLL (1832–1898)

The tool for accomplishing this noble aim is primarily the written word. Books should be the nourishment of the mind — literally.

> "Some books are to be tasted, others to
> be swallowed, and some few are to be
> chewed and digested."
> — FRANCIS BACON (1561–1626)

> "A few books thoroughly digested, rather
> than hundreds but gargled in the mouth."
> — FRANCIS OSBORNE (1593–1659)

That is just the problem with education, too much gargling and not enough digesting.

> "There's more ado to interpret interpretations,
> than to interpret things: and more books upon
> books, than upon any other subject."
> — MICHEL DE MONTAIGNE (1533–1592)

The Alexandrian Library was the greatest educational institution of its time. It had the effect of stultifying Greek learning. That strangest of entities, the scholar, instead of advancing knowledge, spent his time in sterile editing and ceaseless commentary. A certain philologist was said to have written 3,500 rolls of commentary, while another scholar studied 1,500 before daring to put pen to parchment.

"Alexandria was familiar with a new type of human being; shy, eccentric, unpractable, incapable of essentials, strangely fierce upon trivialities of literary detail, as bitterly jealous of the colleague within as of the unlearned without — the Scholarly Man."
    —H.G. WELLS (1866–1946)

Preserve us from this damnable tribe.

"If I were founding a university — and I say it with all the seriousness of which I am capable — I would first found a smoky room; then when I had a little more money in hand I would found a dormitory; then after that, or more probably with it, a decent reading room and a library. After that, if I still had money left over that I couldn't use, I would hire a professor and get some textbooks."
    —STEPHEN LEACOCK (1869–1944)

"It is part of the decency of scholars that whenever they return from meals to their study, washing should invariably preclude reading."
    —RICHARD DE BURY (1287–1345)

A good education is supposed to bring to the student a lifelong appreciation of books and reading.

"O celestial gift of divine liberality.... In books cherubim expand their wings, that the soul of the student may ascend and look around from pole to pole."
    —RICHARD DE BURY (1287–1345)

But sadly, this is too often the exception rather than the rule.

"Popular education ... has produced a
vast population able to read but unable
to distinguish what is worth reading."
— GEORGE MACAULAY TREVELYAN
(1876–1962)

"Would your son be a sot or dunce,
Lascivious, headstrong, or all of these at
once;
Train him in public with a mob of boys,
Childish in mischief only and in noise,
Else of mannish growth, and five in ten
In infidelity and lewdness men.
There shall he learn, ere sixteen winters
old
That authors are most useful pawned or
sold;
That pedantry is all that schools impart
But taverns teach the knowledge of the
heart."
— WILLIAM COWPER (1731–1800)

It is possible to receive a so-called education and never read.

"What I admire in the order to which you
belong is that they do live in the air, that they
excel in the athletic sports, that they only
speak one language; and that they never read.
This is not a complete education, but it is the
highest education since the Greek."
— BENJAMIN DISRAELI (1804–1881)

It is easy to read and not be educated. Having many educational books on your shelf is not always a good thing.

"The enormous multiplication of books in each
branch of knowledge is one of the greatest evils
of this age; since it presents one of the most
serious obstacles to the acquisition of correct
information, by throwing in the reader's way
piles of lumber in which he must painfully
grope for the scraps of useful material,
peradventure interspersed."
— EDGAR ALLAN POE (1809–1849)

To have read all those educational books is even less desirable.

"The bookful blockhead ignorantly read,
with loads of learned lumber in his head."
— ALEXANDER POPE (1688–1744)

"Learning hath gained most by those
books which the printers have lost."
— THOMAS FULLER (1608–1661)

Great learning does little or nothing to foster a love of literature.

"Our American professors like their
literature clear, cold and very dead."
— SINCLAIR LEWIS (1885–1951)

"To be able to distinguish between a
badly- and well-written book is not
enough; a professor of literature can do
that occasionally."
— GEORGE MOORE (1852–1933)

It has to come naturally.

"Scholars who are worth anything at all never
know what is called a 'hard grind' or what 'bitter study' means. They merely love books and
read because they cannot help themselves."
— LIN YUTANG (1895–1976)

The only true education is self-education.

"A man ought to read just as inclination leads
him, for what he reads as a task will do him
little good. A young man should read five
hours in a day, and so many acquire a great
deal of knowledge."
— SAMUEL JOHNSON (1709–1784)

"A man should keep his little brain attic
stocked with all the furniture he is likely
to use, and the rest he can put away in
the lumber room of his library, where he
can get it if he wants it."
      — SIR ARTHUR CONAN DOYLE
      (1859–1930)

"With half an hour's reading in bed every
night as a steady practice, the busiest
man can get a fair education before the
plasma sets in the periganglionic spaces of
his grey cortex."
      — SIR WILLIAM OSLER (1849–1919)

Conclusion

"We may live without poetry, music and art;
We may live without conscience, and live without heart;
We may live without friends; we may live without books,
But civilized man cannot live without cooks."
     —EDWARD BULWER, EARL OF LYTTON (1831–1891)

Indices

"Any simpleton may write a book,
but it requires high skill to make
an index."
 — ROSSITER JOHNSON
 (1840–1931)

 "Albert Naquet once said to me
 with true French flavour: 'A book
 without an index is as incomplete
 as an eunuch.'"
  — THEODORE STANTON
  (1851–1925)

"Of course one has to have an index. Authors themselves would
prefer not to have any. Having
none would save the trouble and
compel reviewers to read the
whole book instead of just the index."
 — STEPHEN LEACOCK
(1869–1944)

 "There are men who pretend to
 understand a book by scouting
 through the index: as if a traveller
 should go about to describe a
 palace when he has seen nothing
 but the privy."
  — JONATHAN SWIFT (1667–1745)

Speaker/Writer Index

Ascham, Roger 79

Bacon, Francis 104
Barrie, James (Sir) 97
Baudelaire, Charles 96
Beecher, Henry Ward 10, 49, 50, 51,
 66
Beerbohm, Max 87
Belloc, Hilaire 5, 97
Benchley, Robert 90, 97, 98
Berenson, Bernard 53
Bible (Ecclesiastes) 37, 103
Bierce, Ambrose 45
Binney, Horace 41
Birrell, Augustine 51
Blair, Robert 103
Blumenthal, W. Hart 10
Braine, John 90, 95
Brautigan, Richard 98
Brook, George Leslie 55
Brown, Thomas 69
Bulwer, Edward (1st Earl of
 Lytton) 109
Burton, John Hill 73
Burton, Robert 103
Bury, Richard de 17, 28, 34, 59, 60,
 61-2, 105
Byron, George Gordon (6th Baron
 Byron) 3

Callimachus 33
Campbell, John 110
Canadian Department of
 Agriculture 49
Carlyle, Thomas 19, 33
Carroll, Lewis 90, 104
Cato, Marcus Porcius (The Elder) 64
Chamfort, Nicholas 38, 97

Chaucer, Geoffrey 53
Chesterfield, Lord (4th Earl of
 Chesterfield) 39, 55
Chesterton, Gilbert Keith 54
Churchill, Winston (Sir) 95
Coleridge, Samuel Taylor 18, 41, 87,
 89, 99
Collins, Larry 28-9
Conan Doyle, Arthur (Sir) 108
Cowper, William 106
Crabbe, George 86-7
Cuppy, Will 90

Davies, Frank 53
Davies, Robertson 19, 20, 37, 52, 88
Dickens, Charles 4, 35, 39
Dimnet, Ernest 91
Diogenes 80
Disraeli, Benjamin 35, 88, 92, 106
D'Israeli, Isaac 61
Dudek, Louis 98
Dunne, Finley Peter 7, 15, 88, 95
Dury, John 25

Ecclesiastes see Bible (Ecclesiastes)
Ellington, Edward Kennedy "Duke" 42
Emerson, Ralph Waldo 5, 10, 27, 41,
 51, 66
Encyclopedia of Anecdotes 39
Erasmus, Desiderus 49

Fadiman, Clifton 79
Ferriar, John 50
Field, Eugene 54
France, Anatole 63
Franklin, Benjamin 38

Froude, James 96
Fulford, Robert 50, 54–5
Fuller, Thomas 107

Galbraith, Georgie Starbuck 77
Gibbon, Edward 53
Gissing, George 53
Goldman, Emma 75
Grahame, Kenneth 11
Green, Martin 19
Griffith, Elizabeth 18

Haines, Helen 23, 27, 36
Haliburton, Thomas Chandler 85
Hamerton, Philip 92
Hare, Augustus William 37
Hare, Julius Charles 37
Hawthorne, Nathaniel 96
Hazlitt, William 41
Hecht, Ben 74
Heine, Heinrich 91
Helps, Arthur (Sir) 91
Henry, William (Duke of
    Gloucester) 40
Herbert, George 64, 65
Holmes, Oliver Wendell 20, 44
Hood, Thomas 37
Howells, William Dean 51
Hubbard, Elbert 35, 46
Hubbard, Frank McKinney "Kin" 64
Hugo, Victor 42
Hunt, Leigh 55, 86

Ibn Tibbon, Juda 28
Ingulf (Abbot of Croyland) 62
Isidore (Bishop of Seville) 11

Johnson, Rossiter 110
Johnson, Samuel 26, 85, 96, 107

Kelland, Clarence Budington 99

King, Stoddard 74
Kipling, Rudyard 42, 43

Lamb, Charles 4, 9, 39, 45, 54, 55,
    59, 65, 66, 89
Lang, Andrew 52, 64
Lapierre, Dominique 28–9
Larkin, Philip 37
Leacock, Stephen 39, 79, 81, 105, 110
Lear, Edward 92
Lee, Gypsy Rose 93
Leo XIII (Pope) 71
Lewis, Sinclair 107
Lictenberg, Georg Christolph 41
Lowell, James Russell 45, 92
Lowry, Malcolm 1
Lucian 37
Luther, Martin 72
Lyly, John 64

Macaulay, Thomas Babington 11
McCord, David T. W. 42
Marlowe, Christopher 44
Marquis, Don 97
Martial 14
Masson, Tom 20
Maugham, William Somerset 80, 90
Mencken, Henry Louis 55
Mifflen, Jessie Beaumont 26
Mizner, Wilson 86
Montaigne, Michel de 75, 104
Moore, George 74, 107
Mottley, John 27
Mowat, Farley 29
Murdoch, Walter 38, 92

Nashe, Thomas 73
Needham, Richard 21, 44, 101
Nesbit, Wilbur Dick 88
Nicholas V (Pope) 63
Nicholson, P. 57
Nietzsche, Friedrich 3, 43, 88
Nordau, Max 98

Omar II (Caliph) 3
Orwell, George 95

Osborne, Francis 104
Osler, William (Sir) 108

Pascal, Blaise 5, 95
Peacock, Thomas Love 5, 38
Pearson, Edmund 44
Peter, Laurence J. 71
Peters, Elizabeth 10
Poe, Edgar Allan 106
Pope, Alexander 63, 107

Robinson, Edward Arlington 65
Rogers, Samuel 45
Rogers, Will 18
Rosenbach, Abraham Simon Wolf
  47
Roux, James 97
Ruskin, John 19, 21, 40

Scott, Walter (Sir) 65
Seneca 14, 81
Shakespeare, William 35, 49, 64, 67,
  74, 83, 103
Shaw, George Bernard 80, 85, 103
Sheridan, Richard Brinsley 3
Smith, Alexander 9
Smith, Goldwin 10
Smith, Horace 10

Smith, Logan Pearsall 45
Stanton, Theodore 110
Steinbeck, John 64
Stevenson, Robert Louis 38,
  85
Strindberg, August 98
Swift, Jonathan 96, 110

Taylor, Bayard 10
Tey, Josephine 29
Thoreau, Henry David 91, 96
Trevelyan, George Macaulay 106
Twain, Mark 4, 20, 37, 38, 72, 80,
  81, 91

UNESCO 31
Uzanne, Louis Octave 50

Van Horne, William (Sir) 81

Waddington, Miriam 75
Wallace, Edgar 74
Ward, Artemus 80
Waugh, Evelyn 4
Webster, John 74
Wells, Carolyn 65, 67

Key Word & Subject Index

Aesop's Fables 36
Alexandria, Library of 13, 34, 104, 105
Alice in Wonderland 29
Apollo, Library of 59
Aristotle 13, 14, 53
Ars Amatoria 71
Assurbanipal 11, 12
Athens 12, 13, 14
Augustus 15, 71
Aurelius, Marcus 59
Austen, Jane 20
Authors 10

Berlioz, Hector 25
Best sellers 45
Bible 16, 36, 72, 73
Books 3, 13, 14, 15, 16, 17, 31–46, 49,
   59, 72, 75, 101, 104; burning of 37,
   44, 69, 73; children and 5, 6, 55, 86;
   covers and appearance of 38, 39, 50,
   54, 66, 74; dangers of 42, 43, 44,
   45, 50, 51, 52, 54, 55, 57, 92, 106,
   107; love of 9, 16, 21, 49–53, 55,
   107; new 44, 45, 90; smell of 9, 43,
   53; students and 60, 61–2, 103, 105,
   107; theft of 17, 25, 52, 57, 61, 63,
   64, 65; value and use of 17, 20, 37–
   40, 42, 46, 61–2, 81, 90, 104, 105;
   women and 41, 53, 87, 88, 89, 90
Bookworms 4, 47–56, 88
Borges, Jorge Luis 25
Borrowing and lending 4, 12, 13, 18,
   28, 57–67
Braine, John 25
Burgandy, Third Duke of 17

Cadmus 33
Caesar, Julius 15

Callimachus 33, 34
Carlyle, Thomas 90
Casanova, Giovanni 25
Caxton, William 36
Censorship 4, 69–76
Charlemagne 85
Chaucer, Geoffrey 36, 80
Chin Shengt'an 75
Cicero 14, 36
Classics 4, 77–81
Codexes 35
Coleridge, Samuel Taylor 66
Congress, Library of 18, 26
Cooks 109
Cooper, James Fenimore 81
Cuneiform 33

Decline and Fall of the Roman
   Empire 40
Deerslayer, The 81
Dictes and Sayings of the
   Philosphres 36
Disraeli, Benjamin 54

Education 4, 86, 101–8
Egypt 11, 12, 34, 59
Encyclopedia Britannica 28–9
Engels, Freidrich 25
Eumenes II 34
Eunuchs 27, 95, 110
Evans, Arthur 25

Faerie Queene 54
Fanny Hill 71
Fielding, Henry 89
First editions 39–40
Franklin, Benjamin 25

Game and Playe of Chesse, The 36
Gibbon, Edward 40, 45
Gilgamesh, The 33
Goethe, Johann Wolfgang Von 25
Gordian the Younger 53
Great Nabu 12
Greece 12, 13, 14, 33, 59, 79
Grimm, Jacob 25
Grimm, Wilhelm 25
Gutenberg, Johannes 53

Hamlet 97
Harems 10, 27, 95
Hieroglyphics 85
Henry I 85
Henry VIII 17
Hesiod 81
Hoover, J. Edgar 25
Huckleberry Finn 72
Hume, David 25, 45

Incunabula 36
Indexes 111
Isabel, Queen of France 17

Joe Miller's Jests 27

Kant, Immanuel 25
Kessem, Abdul 16
King Solomon's Mines 92

Lady Chatterley's Lover 71
Leibniz, Gottfried Wilhelm Von 25
Librarians 3, 12, 14, 19, 23-9, 59,
    101; India 28-9; Monastic 34, 59;
    Pakistan 28-9; university 25
Libraries 3, 7-21; circulating 3, 18,
    19, 91; Islamic 16, 60; Monastic 16,
    17, 28, 59; private 13, 14, 17, 108;
    public 11, 13, 15, 19, 20, 59, 66, 67,
    75; university 60

Library patrons 11, 18, 20, 23, 25, 26,
    59, 60
Longfellow, Henry Wadsworth 25

McLuhan, Marshall 53
Magna Carta 85
Malory, Thomas (Sir) 36
Manchester Free Library 19
Mao Tse-Tung 25
Medici, Cosimo de 17
Medici, Lorenzo de 17
Mesopotamia 11, 59, 71
Middle Ages 16, 17, 25, 60, 61, 62,
    63, 86
Morte d'Arthur, Le 36, 79

Naquet, Albert 110
New College Library 60
Newfoundland 26
Niccoli, Niccolò 17
Nicolas V 17
Ninevah, Library of 11, 12
Non-Books 45

Ouyang Hsiu 99
Ovid 71
Ozymandius *see* Ramses II

Palimpsests 34
Pamela 89
Paper 35
Papyrus 13, 15, 33, 34,
    35
Parchment 16, 34, 35
Pergamum, Library of
    34
Pisistratus 13
Plato 13
Pliny the Younger 15
Pollio, Asinius 15
Prefaces 1
Printing 35, 72, 73
Ptolemy II 13, 34

Quotations 5

Ramses II 12, 25
Reading 4, 12, 14, 18, 42, 44, 50, 54, 55, 83–92, 106, 108
Recuyell of the Historyes of Troye 36
Richardson, Samuel 89
Rome 14, 15, 25, 33, 59

Sade, Marquis de 72
Sartor Resartus 90
Scribes 13, 16
Sex 10, 47, 71, 74, 75, 90, 98
Shamela 89
Shaw, George Bernard 26
Shelley, Percy Bysshe 12
Siculus, Diodorous 12
Stationers' Company 73, 74
Stoics 14
Strindberg, August 25
Sumeria 33

Tasmanian Parliamentary Library 92
Thebes, Library of 12, 25, 33
Toronto 75
Tropic of Capricorn 71

Ulysses 71
Ur, Royal Library of 25

Vatican Library 17

Writing 4, 49, 72, 93–9
Wuthering Heights 29

Zola, Émile 98